The British Association
for Shooting & Conservation

HANDBOOK OF SI

THE SPORTING SHOTGUN

The British Association
for Shooting & Conservation

BASC

HANDBOOK OF SHOOTING
THE SPORTING SHOTGUN

SWAN·HILL
PRESS

ACKNOWLEDGEMENTS

The British Association for Shooting and Conservation gratefully acknowledges the following:
Clay Pigeon Shooting Association (C.P.S.A.) for their kind permission to reproduce notes on how to shoot a moving target in Appendix 5; the British Proof Authorities for permission to reproduce British proof marks and the Spanish Proof Authorities for permission to reproduce Spanish proof marks in Appendix 3; Ian Hepburn for technical advice and contribution to the quarry identification section; and members of BASC staff past and present who have all contributed knowledge and expertise.

ILLUSTRATIONS

Full colour illustrations of quarry species and black and white line drawings, unless otherwise acknowledged, by John Paley; photographs by Adrian Horgan; drawings of gundogs in Chapter 10 by Ann Seward; distribution maps and shooting-season drawings in Chapter 6 by Ian Hepburn.

First published in the UK in 1983
This edition published 2000
by Swan Hill Press
Second impression 2001

British Library Cataloguing-in-Publication Data
A catalogue record for this book
is available from the British Library

ISBN 1 84037 165 X

The information in this book is true and complete to the best of our knowledge. All recommendations are made without any guarantee on the part of the publisher, who also disclaims any liability incurred in connection wth the use of this data or specific details.

Printed in Singapore by Kyodo Co (S'pore) Pte Ltd

Swan Hill Press

an imprint of Quiller Publishing Ltd
Wykey House, Wykey, Shrewsbury SY4 1JA, England
Website: www.swanhillbooks.com
Email: info@quillerbooks.com

Contents

Foreword

by HRH The Prince Philip, Duke of Edinburgh
Patron of the British Association for Shooting and Conservation

To the uninitiated almost every leisure occupation appears to be rather simple, if not childish. Oscar Wilde's comment about foxhunting that it was a case of the 'unspeakable in full pursuit of the uneatable' reflects this deep-rooted suspicion of anything strange or partly understood.

There is obviously much more to these occupations than is apparent at first sight. The fisherman may look as if he is just dangling a hook in the water, but anyone with experience knows that this appearance is deceptive. Golf may look as if it is just a matter of hitting a little white ball about the country and walking after it, but the volume of media coverage of golf tournaments and the shelves of books on the game suggest that its challenge fascinates a great many people.

Shooting is no exception. In fact, as this book makes clear, in order to enjoy it and to practise it sensibly and safely, needs a great deal of knowledge and skill in a number of different departments.

The first rule of sporting shooting is that it must always follow the principles of good husbandry.

Farmers don't eat their seed corn and cattlemen see that they maintain their stock of breeding cows: likewise, responsible shooting people always remember that there will be another season next year.

The second rule is that shooting practised thoughtlessly and irresponsibly is almost bound to result in cruelty. The intention must always be to kill cleanly and inflict the least possible suffering on the quarry. Therefore the chapters on Behaviour in the Field and Codes of Practice are extremely important.

How to achieve these ends, and a great deal more extremely useful guidance and information, has been collected together in this book which I am quite sure will be of the greatest value to young and old, beginners or old hands alike.

The British Association for Shooting and Conservation

Stanley Duncan, a Humber estuary wildfowler, founded the Association in 1908 in response to the growing threats to wildfowl and their habitat. From its inception until the 1950s the Wildfowlers' Association of Great Britain and Ireland (WAGBI) remained a modest but genuinely successful and respected body.

But growth was essential if sporting shooting was to be adequately protected. Recognising that strength is in numbers, the concerted effort to recruit membership resulted in the title being changed, first to WAGBI – for Wildfowling and Rough-shooting, and later to WAGBI – for Shooting and Conservation. Additional strength was provided when the Gamekeepers' Association of the United Kingdom, itself founded in 1900, amalgamated with WAGBI.

Membership support continued to grow but many thousands of people interested in shooting still could not identify with the Association. So it was that, in 1981, the Association changed its title to The BRITISH ASSOCIATION for SHOOTING and CONSERVATION in order fully to represent sporting shooting. Details of membership benefits and advantages may be obtained by writing to the BASC, Marford Mill, Rossett, Wrexham, LL12 0HL.

Proficiency Award Scheme

WHY HAS THE PROFICIENCY AWARD SCHEME BEEN INTRODUCED?

Traditionally, the Association has placed a great deal of emphasis on education and training. Some time ago the Education Sub-Committee produced a set of Codes of Practice for the sport to guide those seeking basic information. This course of action was undertaken because we believe that as an Association we have a duty to encourage high standards of safety, sportsmanship and courtesy among those who enjoy the legitimate sport of shooting. Following the Codes of Practice series we have established a Proficiency Award Scheme on a purely voluntary basis which offers members and non members a way of improving their knowledge.

The primary purpose of this Handbook for sporting shotgun shooting is to teach shotgun safety, sportsmanship and courtesy. There are also other objectives, such as to teach country lores and traditions, the law relating to shooting and generally to enable those who take part in the sport to derive far greater enjoyment in the knowledge that they are conducting themselves according to acceptable standards of behaviour in the shooting field.

Much of the criticism which is levelled against shooting sports is as a direct result of either misunderstanding or of bad behaviour witnessed in the field. The rights and privileges of sportsmen to continue to enjoy their sport and the satisfaction of conserving the countryside and wildlife depends very much on the behaviour of all shooting people. They will be judged by their attitude and behaviour.

The social structure of the shooting community has altered considerably in the last few years and there are many now who wish to take up the sport, or indeed who have entered it, but have no real knowledge of shooting, of the lores and traditions of the countryside, or of the quarry species they pursue and of the management needs of those species.

The Proficiency Award Scheme has therefore been introduced to give everyone who shoots a practical means of attaining the BASC Ideal – 'That all who shoot lawfully in Britain conduct themselves according to the highest standards of safety, sportsmanship and courtesy, with full respect for their quarry and a practical interest in wildlife conservation and the wellbeing of the countryside.'

WHAT IS IT?

The Scheme is designed to provide a basic course of instruction for anyone interested in this traditional country sport of shooting.

WHAT IS IT FOR?

The Scheme is intended as a practical and enjoyable way for participants in the sport to:
1. Achieve self confidence.
2. Know of, and act on, high standards of safety, sportsmanship and courtesy.
3. Increase their overall knowledge of, and skills in, the sport.
4. Show that they have taken their sport seriously.

WHO CAN TAKE PART?

The course is open to everyone over the age of 14 who has an interest in live quarry shooting with a shotgun.
Newcomers to the sport will benefit most, but experienced shooters who wish to broaden their knowledge will enjoy the course and will have the PAS Certificate and Badge to prove their expertise.

WHAT DOES THE COURSE CONSIST OF?

The course is based on the information contained in 'The Handbook of Shooting' and is made up of a series of informal talks and demonstrations. These are usually given by guest speakers, who are experts in their field and cover a range of subjects, including:

Shotgun safety, shotguns and cartridges, gun maintenance, shooting law and correct behaviour, game and rough shooting, wildfowling, quarry identification, shoot management and the use of gundogs.

Plus there is always time for questions and discussion.

Although marksmanship is not tested, simple written and practical assessments lead to the award of the PAS (non live firing) certificate and badge.

The PAS Award is not only something to be proud of, but it can also be useful proof of your knowledge and responsibility in many other circumstances.

HOW DO I GET ON A COURSE?

The PAS is organised at different venues all around the British Isles by experienced shots, trained by BASC. These are known as Honorary Education Officers or HEOs.

The course is run by colleges who employ HEOs to deliver the course. BASC is the awarding body and does therefore not run any of these courses themselves.

The courses are either run over one or two weekends or on several evenings, plus a daytime practical session.

The Scheme offers a chance to enjoy broadening your knowledge of shooting or to perhaps learn about it for the first time. In either case, you will learn about the 'BASC Ideal'.

THE BASC IDEAL

'That all who shoot lawfully in Britain conduct themselves according to the highest standards of safety, sportsmanship and courtesy, with full respect for their quarry and a practical interest in wildlife conservation and the well being of the countryside.'

For details of colleges that offer the course:
Contact the Education and Training Department at the British Association for Shooting and Conservation, Marford Mill, Rossett, Wrexham, LL12 0HL. Tel. 01244 - 573000.

Shooting and Conservation I

INTRODUCTION

Hunters have been conserving wildlife since the creation of the Royal Hunting Forests in Norman times. Though man has been modifying nature for more than 2000 years, land management for the conservation of wildlife is hardly 100 years old. Until around 1900, when land began to be managed specifically to protect its wildlife, it could be said that Britain's diverse animals and plants survived by accident rather than design. Selective shooting has certainly played its part in that survival. Many people may see shooting and conservation as a conflict in terms, but shooting of quarry species depends upon successful breeding populations of birds and animals, which in turn need a suitable habitat.

It is a fundamental aspect of sportsmanship that the pursuit of the quarry is undertaken with safety, courtesy, respect for the quarry and the countryside and without endangering other people. Shooting cannot take place without affecting the countryside as a whole and people who shoot should be aware of the implications of both their own actions and of other pressures on the environment.

Modern farming techniques, increased leisure time and improved means of travel from urban areas have brought increasing pressures onto the countryside and its wildlife. Those who shoot should have a basic knowledge of issues relating to the countryside and its wildlife; without such knowledge sportsmen bring discredit to the sport and pose yet another threat to its future.

ACCESS AND
SHOOT
MANAGEMENT

Access to land is achieved through public rights of way or by permission of the land owner. Those who shoot require the permission of the owner of the shooting rights. Under most circumstances, anyone in possession of a firearm must have the relevant certificate issued by the police. If in doubt, contact the Firearms section of BASC.

CONSERVATION
CONCEPTS

Conservation does not mean neglect. Some people see conservation as leaving nature to look after itself. Wildlife and game conservation involves the protection, management and wise use of plants, animals and their environment. The next section explains certain conservation concepts.

HABITAT

Habitat is the environment that supplies everything wildlife needs to sustain healthy populations. Different wildlife species require particular habitats. Habitats are classified into broadly distinctive types according to their location, flora and fauna, physical characteristics and geology, i.e. lowland deciduous woodland. Each habitat type provides the food, cover, water and space for the wildlife living there.

HABITAT
MANAGEMENT

The foundation stone of wildlife management is the provision of suitable habitats. In Britain man has changed the face of nature through agriculture and hunting for thousands of years so that much of the wildlife we enjoy today is a result of man's intervention.

Aspects of the habitat that can be managed are the availability of food and water and the provision of cover or open spaces. Countryside which provides a mixture of habitats is clearly desirable since it can support a greater variety of species. It is also important to bear in mind that each wildlife species occupies a unique place in the environment. If a particular habitat changes in character or is altered by management some species may do well and others decline. Inappropriate management of a woodland habitat for pheasants or ponds for mallards, for example, can have a negative effect on other species.

SPECIES
MANAGEMENT

Some wildlife can harm other species and their habitat if not controlled. This is particularly true of non native species which are now adapted to the British countryside and can often harm native plants and animals. Where populations get too large or individuals cause specific problems, nature reserve managers and game managers have to act to maintain a balance.

Examples of where control may be necessary include; populations of deer which have grown to the extent that they are severely damaging habitat, control of magpies and crows that prey on game and songbird chicks and eggs and the control of non native mink that can severely reduce wildfowl and water vole populations.

The intention is always to maintain a balance rather than to remove any species.

COMMUNITIES

A community is a group of plants or animals existing in a habitat, usually dependant in some way on one another for survival. Only by maintaining entire communities is it likely that the complex and the interdependent needs of different species can be satisfied.

SUCCESSION

Left alone, nature changes habitats through a process called 'succession'. As a lake fills with silt it gradually becomes a pond, then a marsh and beyond this dry land and a forest. Similarly, moorland left to nature would become covered in scrub and eventually revert to woodland.

Many of the most important wildlife communities in Britain are of an early successional stage and much effort of conservationists is taken up in suspending i.e. coppicing woodland, in order to promote these early successional stages.

COMPETITION

Plants and animals compete for the same resources, usually food or space. The diversity of a particular habitat and its species is often affected by competition for the same food resource by the species present. An example of competition is that between red squirrels and grey squirrels. Grey squirrels feed on unripe hazel nuts and acorns and therefore harvest the hazel nuts before they are ready for red squirrels that prefer the ripened nuts. This leads to reduced feeding opportunity for red squirrels, causing them, dependent on other factors, to decline.

In this case therefore habitat management would involve improving conditions for the more vulnerable species i.e. the red squirrel. This could be done by, for example, not planting oak tees, on whose acorns grey squirrels thrive, in areas where grey squirrels are present.

PREDATION

Predation can be defined as one animal being 'preyed upon' or acting as a food resource, for another. For example, hedgehogs, which are preyed upon by badgers are only common in areas where badgers are scarce, such as urban settlements where badger predation is low. It has been shown that by reducing dominant predator species the surrounding communities can benefit from an increase in diversity. In game management it has been shown that by reducing the numbers of predatory species, such as corvids (crows, magpies etc.), game managers increase the diversity of woodland species such as song birds.

RESEARCH AND MONITORING

Habitat requirements of many species are still not well known or understood. Research is required to provide an analysis of the various methods of managing the countryside for game and wildlife and for providing practical solutions. Monitoring is a fundamental part of research and some form of monitoring should be carried out by anyone managing land. Monitoring an area enables the game manager to assess the success of management schemes.

MODERN CONSERVATION

The late 19th century and early 20th century saw the formation of both government and voluntary conservation organisations such as the Nature Conservancy Council (now English Nature), Scottish Natural Heritage and the Countryside Council for Wales, RSPB and the British Trust for Ornithology, in response to a growing concern for wildlife. BASC was formed as WAGBI in 1908 because of wildfowlers' concerns over threats to wetlands.

Initially, the majority of government and voluntary conservation organisations channelled their efforts into nature reserves, i.e. sites managed specifically for certain species of wildlife and plants. In many instances the reserves were treated like museums rather than living, changing environments. More recently conservation ideas have changed and many now believe that the future of conservation lies not just in reserves but in the rural land outside them. It is also now generally accepted that for conservation to work in the wider countryside it must involve local communities and interest groups.

An important step in promoting nature conservation outside nature reserves was the 1992 convention on Biological Diversity at Rio de Janeiro, Brazil. The Convention, which was attended by more than 150 countries from around the world was called to discuss the world wide loss of 'variety' within animal and plant communities (known as 'biodiversity'). This 'variety' refers to species variety, e.g. goshawk, sparrowhawk and kestrel, and habitat variety e.g. woodland, heath land and grassland. Following the biodiversity convention, governments agreed to draw up Biodiversity Action Plans. The UK Biodiversity Action Plan Steering Group report, which was published in January 1994, identified key species/habitats considered most at risk and separate strategies were completed for each one. Local Biodversity Action Plans are being developed to reflect the local needs of wildlife and their habitat. Sportsmen must also endeavour to become involved in broader issues concerning wildlife conservation and biodiversity in order to promote game and wildlife and their habitat.

The following broad habitat types identified by the UK Biodiversity Action Plan Steering Group report are often where sporting shooting management takes place and where those sportsmen can contribute to biodiversity conservation: lowland broadleaved woodland, native pine woods, hedgerows, arable field margins, upland heath land, open water, fens/reedbeds, estuaries and coastal areas (see detailed descriptions of habitat types below).

SHOOTING AS AN INCENTIVE FOR CONSERVATION

The shooting community has direct influence over vast areas of country-side. Shooting provides an incentive for the retention of habitats, such as native woodlands, ponds and moorland. Heather moorland is managed for grouse; woodlands, hedgerows and field margins for pheasant and partridge; inland ponds and lakes as well as saltmarshes in coastal areas, are managed for duck and geese.

While the primary objective of such management is often to maintain and increase quarry populations, the maintenance of habitats enables sportsmen to conserve and enhance the overall population and range of native non-quarry species and the quality and range of habitats of benefit to much other wildlife.

Research by Cobham Resource Consultants 1997 shows that habitat creation was two to three times greater in landscapes positively managed for shooting. The Game Management Project (1994) found that new woodland planting occurs on 68% of holdings where pheasants are released, compared with only 19% on holdings which do not release pheasants, ride management is seven times more likely to occur, coppicing nine times more likely to occur and shrub planting four times more likely to occur on holdings with game management interests.

Examples of the beneficial effects of game interest include the use of conservation headlands on the margins of cereal fields which greatly improve gamebird rearing, whilst also increasing the biodiversity of butterflies, songbirds and wildflowers.

The survival of heather moorland is also closely associated with grouse shooting and benefits breeding waders such as golden plover and dunlin together with birds of prey such as hen harrier and merlin. Financial returns from shooting provide a valuable incentive for habitat conservation, but it is not just about money. Enjoyable sport in a self managed and wildlife rich landscape is often the only return sought by those who shoot.

LOCAL INVOLVEMENT IN CONSERVATION

A fundamental principle of biodiversity conservation is local involvement. The shooting community represent a local 'hands on' conservation resource which is additional to that represented by government bodies and voluntary organisations. Conservation and land management carried out by sportsmen extend from the restoration of village ponds right through to management of National Nature Reserves.

In England, BASC affiliated clubs alone have management influence

7

over 105,000ha of land, of which approximately 7% are Sites of Special Scientific Interest (SSSI). On such sites, clubs together with the help of BASC site management plans which help to integrate shooting interests with active management for nature conservation.

Shoot managers are often involved in species protection programmes and many warden important wildlife sites including National Nature Reserves (NNRs). The nests of rare birds such as red kites are protected by gamekeepers under schemes like 'Eggwatch'. Other schemes such as 'Poacher Watch' help prevent illegal hare and deer poaching. On the coast, wildfowling clubs own and protect land where rare nesting birds, such as the little tern, breed.

PAYING FOR
CONSERVATION Management for conservation is a costly business. Today, more than ever, people are showing an interest in conserving our natural heritage. The Government funds NNRs and provides financial support to encourage good management on SSSIs. A wide range of grant schemes are also available for conservation management, but funds are limited.

There will always be a reliance on voluntary organisations and individuals to manage the wider countryside and maintain its nature conservation interest. Government conservation efforts in the absence of country sports would cost taxpayers millions of pounds. In the 1997 Cobham Report countryside sports were shown to generate more than £6.2 billion.

Only two per cent of Britain's 22 million hectares of countryside is under the protection of nature reserves, 88% is under the control of farmers and other landowners. In total more than half the UK has shooting over it. Voluntary conservation, by those interested in shooting, therefore, is vital in helping to ensure the conservation of the wider countryside and the viability of the rural economy.

WILDLIFE
HABITAT TRUST The Wildlife Habitat Trust was set up in 1986 to assist in shooting's vital conservation role. It is an independent fund dedicated to the acquisition, creation and management of wildlife habitats for the joint benefit of conservation and shooting. The Trust has supported projects on nationally and internationally important sites such as the Norfolk Broads, North Kent Marshes, Hamford Water in Essex, the Ribble Estuary in Lancashire and the Ouse Washes in Cambridgeshire. A portion of funds raised also goes to international conservation projects including management programmes in the Baltic States and Turkey. These areas are part of the birds' annual migratory routes.

The following section provides information on the conservation importance of several common habitat types over which shooting takes place and explores ways in which the sportsman contributes to conservation.

MOORLANDS

The main features of Britain's upland landscapes are mountains, open heaths and moors. Uplands can be broadly defined as land above 240 metres. Moorlands, typically open expanses of heather or grasses, cover 1.7

million hectares. Moorland areas are mainly found in the west and north of England and Wales, and throughout Scotland and Northern Ireland.

The conservation value of moorland is high and the UK Biodiversity Action Plan recommends that moorland should be maintained in extent, range and quality, but it is increasingly under threat. Moorland has declined as a result of both afforestation and agricultural improvement. In 1983 it was estimated that loss of moorland had been running at an average rate of 5,000 hectares per annum over the previous 30 years.

Well-managed moorlands can support a range of plant and animal species. Moorland vegetation is dependent on altitude, soil type, weather and exposure. Such habitats are not found in such profusion anywhere else in the world.

Moors where grasses dominate are a result of heavy grazing by sheep. Where bracken flourishes, little else survives.

Many moorland birds of conservation importance are closely associated with the upland vegetation. Young heather is the staple diet of the red grouse. The bilberry shoots and leaves feed the black grouse and ptarmigan. Berries found on moorlands are eaten by ring ouzels. Short vegetation is favoured for nesting by golden plover, lapwing and greenshank whilst hen harrier, merlin, short-eared owl, snipe and curlew all like taller vegeation.

Moors support many insects, which in turn feed birds and other animals. Reptiles such as lizards and adders thrive on moorlands as do larger animals such as stoats and red deer.

THE ROLE OF
THE SPORTSMAN

Many see the value of moorland in its naturalness, but historically management of moors has been determined almost entirely by their use for farming, forestry and game management. Nearly one third of our moorland (nearly ½ million hectares) is managed for red grouse shooting. Red grouse feed principally on heather, needing a variety of growth stages for food and nesting cover. Sportsmen manage heather by the rotational burning of small patches generally over a fifteen-year cycle, to provide optimum conditions for the birds.

Burning benefits many other species including more than fifty species of ground beetle. Weevils favour younger heather whilst older heather has the highest invertebrate diversities. When gamekeepers are not looking after moorland areas, bird numbers can decline. Control of crows and foxes reduces predation on grouse and their nests. Burning, together with predator control, benefits other nesting birds, such as the black grouse, lapwing, and skylark.

Occasionally, the only reason moorlands have not been lost under blanket afforestation or to overgrazing by livestock, has been the economic return from grouse shooting. Deer can also overgraze and damage moorland and shooting is a vital control method. Populations of red deer in Scotland are increasing and the need for management is widely accepted. Trained stalkers are used by many large estates and conservation bodies, to reduce deer densities. In so doing shooting benefits conservation and gives an economic return.

Grouse shooting and deer stalking are two crucial components of the conservation of our threatened moorland habitats. Recognition of this is widespread throughout the conservation world.

WOODLANDS

Woodland can be generally defined as any area dominated by trees and shrubs. The British Isles were extensively wooded following the last ice age. Neolithic man began the clearance of trees to create land for cultivation. Now only around 10 per cent of our land area is covered with trees. Small relics of ancient woodland cover still remain today, but the majority of our woodland is semi-natural. The conservation value of woodland is dependent on the type and composition of tree species present and the influence of man's past management.

Ancient woodland, origins of which can be traced back to the last ice age, is the most scarce woodland habitat and highly valued by conservationalists because of its historical interest and species richness. Ancient Caledonian pine forests found in Scotland are relics of the upland tree cover from post ice age Britain. They provide the home for the rare capercaillie as well as birds such as crested tits and crossbills.

Semi-natural woodland, predominantly native species of broad-leaved and coniferous trees and shrubs, is perhaps the most familiar form of woodland in Britain. This type of woodland has almost always been planted by man and has been extensively managed. Its conservation interest varies with the tree species present. The UK Biodiversity Action Plan recommends that ancient and semi-natural woodland should be maintained. The plan recommends that such woods should be expanded by planting new native woodland in adjacent areas.

The ground flora of ancient and semi-natural woodland is made up of familiar plant species such as bluebells and wood anemones. Many of our woodland butterflies (such as fritillaries) depend on the ground flora growing in rides and glades of semi-natural woodland.

Commercial conifer forests are often considered 'unnatural' woodlands. These are often stands of a single species, producing a quickly maturing timber crop to provide an early financial return for the landowner. Whilst such areas do support a range of wildlife, they lack the habitat diversity found in ancient and semi-natural woodland. The UK Biodiversity Steering Group Report recommends that coniferous woodland should be restructured and diversified to improve its conservation potential.

Woodlands can support a large number of bird species, from woodpeckers, which need older trees for nesting and feeding, to great tits, blue tits, wrens and chaffinches, all common for woodland birds. As with many other species, mammals have specific requirements from woodlands. Woodland provides the sheltered banks where badgers prefer to excavate their setts. Dormice are increasingly rare in Britain and dependant on a range of woodland plants from hazel to honeysuckle for all the year round food. The red squirrel is now largely restricted to coniferous woodlands in northern parts of the British Isles. Woodland types in all areas will support our native deer species.

Woodlands in Britain have a long history of management by man for timber and game. In the Victorian and Edwardian era the establishment of large sporting estates led to the planting of extensive areas of woodland as game cover. This contribution by sportsmen continues today, with many new woodlands planted for shoot purposes.

Research for the Forestry Commission has revealed that more than 60 per cent of people planting woodlands with grant aid have shooting interests as their primary objective. In addition to planting, shooting provides an incentive for the appropriate management of woodlands in ways which benefit wildlife as well as game.

Pheasants are birds of the woodland edge and their management requires the creation and enhancement of habitats at the edge of and within woodlands involving cutting of glades and rides. This favours woodland plants such as primroses, bluebells and violets. Open areas also benefit insects such as butterflies, the very rare Duke of Burgundy fritillary continues to be found in woodlands in Sussex which are managed for shooting. Shooting is also as important in forest conservation, encouraging managers of conifer plantations to manage less intensively for timber and more for game and wildlife. Plantations that have various stages of growth will attract a range of species, including short-eared owls and pipits in new plantings and goldcrests and black game in thickets and clearings.

Sportsmen have a crucial role in managing deer populations in woodlands. Deer can cause considerable damage to timber, trees and the wider conservation interests of woodland areas. They are liable to spread out to surrounding agricultural land, thus damaging crops. Shooting is often the only way to limit such damage whilst also providing valuable income and maintaing a healthy deer population.

WETLANDS

Ponds are a familiar and popular conservation resource. Natural springs, ponds and lakes occur mainly in the northwest, as a result of glacial action, impervious rocks and a lot of rain. Most of the ponds of Britain, however, are man made, by damming or diverting springs, flooding pits used for clay, sand, peat or gravel extraction and by digging into ground water to provide water for stock or irrigation purposes. Nationally ponds are estimated to support 300 plant species and 50 per cent of the breeding fish species. Often fringed by trees, emergent and bankside vegetation, these areas provide a safe nesting haven for birds such as duck, grebes and moorhens.

From the uplands of Britain, streams and rivers flow into the lowlands and on into the sea. Around all these water sources, fresh water marshes, bogs, reed beds and wet pasture can exist.

Rivers can vary immensely in their plant and wildlife value. They differ in their flow, nutrient content, silt loads and other geological and biological factors. Often upland rivers tend to have a stony substrate and little vegetation supporting fish like trout and birds such as dippers. Lowland rivers flow more slowly, meandering through valleys with lush vegetation. Submerged plants shelter many fish species such as rudd and pike, whilst wildfowl can be found nesting in vegetation along banks. Steep river banks provide nesting sites for birds such as kingfishers and sandmartins.

Ponds support a huge range of animals and plants. Pondweed, reeds and rushes provide habitat and food for invertebrates such as pond snails, water beetles and caddis flies whilst providing cover for amphibians, such as newts, fish and the birds that eat them. Water voles and otters depend on rivers and otters will often use many of the habitats around a river from its upland source to the sea.

The flooding of grasslands around rivers and ponds creates wet pasture and fresh water marshes. This is important feeding and breeding habitat for birds such as redshank, snipe and rarities like ruff and black tailed godwits. Bogs and reed beds form in areas of permanently water logged land. Bogs in upland areas comprising sphagnum mosses, sedges and insect eating plants such as sundews, provide breeding sites for waders such as greenshank. Reed beds provide important nesting habitats for birds such as reed bunting and the rare bittern, as well as being popular resting sites for migrating birds such as swallows.

Wetlands are a threatened habitat. Land improvement for agriculture often means drainage schemes. Increasing water abstraction, particularly in the south east of England, has lowered the water table and caused conservation problems. Ponds and wetlands are often seen as economically unproductive and are filled in for development purposes. Ponds left unmanaged will silt up, eventually becoming scrub and woodland and of no value to wetland plants and animals.

ESTUARIES

Estuaries are formed where rivers meet the sea. The daily movement of the tide and the mixing of fresh and salt waters give estuaries complex and varying habitats and wildlife. There are some 163 estuaries which have been identified around the coast of the UK. Estuaries vary in size, the largest being the Wash at 660,000 hectares.

Estuaries support a wide range of wildlife and are made up of a diverse mosaic of sub-tidal and intertidal habitats. Even the smaller estuaries may have mudflats, sandflats, saltmarshes, shingles, rocky shores, sand dunes and grazing marshes. Saltmarshes are an important food resource and breeding ground for many birds. Mudflats are also a major part of the estuary ecosystem, supporting vast numbers of invertebrates on which fish and many nationally and internationally important waterfowl feed.

Many waders, wildfowl and seabirds depend almost entirely on estuaries at certain times of the year. Birds that breed in the Arctic or Siberia crowd onto Britain's estuaries in winter. Others use them as resting areas before flying south to spend winter in Africa or elsewhere in Europe and returning north to breed in spring. Estuaries are of particular importance for their international populations of breeding birds such as redshank and ringed plover. Estuaries also support many species of fish, amphibians such as the endangered natterjack toad and mammals such as otters, seals and dolphins.

Extensive estuarine areas are under threat. Since Roman times they have been subject to interference by man when land started to be claimed for farming in the Thames Estuary. Man's use of estuaries nearly always affects wildlife. The list is long: sea defences and harbours, bridges, barrages, road schemes and industrial development, as well as recreation. Conservationists and sportsmen are aware of these potential threats, some old, many current or new. They work together to manage and protect the coast. The UK Biodiversity Action Plan recommends that extent and quality of estuarine habitats (and estuarine communities) should be maintained and enhanced.

THE ROLE OF
THE SPORTSMAN

Ponds, wetlands and estuaries all contribute to the sporting interests of wildfowlers and other shooting people.

Ponds provide the sportsman with an opportunity to shoot flighting duck, principally mallard and teal, but on larger, deeper ponds, pochard and goldeneye. Whilst typically, a pond is not shot over more than ten times in a season sportsmen are some of the most avid pond creators and managers.

An ideal pond for shooting contains all the features of a perfect conservation pond; that is, shallow margins, lots of vegetation, and islands for nesting birds. For relatively few shooting opportunities each year, the benefit to wildlife is considerable.

Whilst wet pasture and marshes have been systematically drained for agriculture and development, their popularity in providing snipe shooting or as resting places for quarry species such as mallard, has ensured that many remnants of valuable marshes remain. Shooting clubs have been involved in the purchase of land on internationally important areas of wetland such as the Ouse Washes, solely to manage the site for waterfowl conservation and provide sport. Once purchased by shooting clubs, the conservation management of the site is secured. The Government, through Environmentally Sensitive Areas, Countryside Stewardship and other agricultural schemes are now encouraging better wetland management in rural areas. Sporting interests, when added to the funds available, act as a great incentive for landowners to restore lost wetland areas and prevent further losses.

Shooters have been responsible for looking after, managing and creating many ponds and wetland areas throughout Britain. Ponds do not look after themselves, but need active management to maintain their wildlife value. Shooters have long recognised this and have been contributing to the sustainable use of wetland habitats for a considerable time.

Wildfowlers have long had an interest in conserving quarry species, duck and geese. In 1960 wildfowlers and conservationists developed a national waterfowl conservation policy which still stands today. It recognised the importance of safeguarding wildfowl populations, whilst allowing controlled wildfowling. Today most wildfowling activity is managed by 200 wildfowling clubs in the UK, comprising 15,000 wildfowlers. These clubs may own the land over which they shoot or own or lease the sporting rights. Where they own land, clubs often enter into agreement with Government Conservation Agencies to manage their land as National Nature Reserves.

Clubs manage habitats to benefit waterfowl and to ensure their shooting is sustainable. For example, on the Dee Estuary areas of saltmarsh are mown to provide feeding for wigeon and pintail within the shooting refuge areas. Many clubs have interests in species protection. On Breydon Water in Norfolk, wildfowlers and local naturalists have built nesting platforms for Britain's rarest breeding coastal bird, the little tern. Often coastal breeding birds are subject to human disturbance and club members will warden colonies to prevent this.

A wildfowling club which owns land on Hamford Water in Essex is paid by the Government to look after a little tern colony. Wildfowl clubs are therefore actively involved in estuary strategies and sit on estuary conservation groups with other conservation bodies and lobby local and national government when threats emerge. Wildfowlers complained to both the UK and European Parliaments after the proposed destruction of Cardiff Bay, an important area of mudflats, by the construction of a barrage.

Clubs regulate their shooting activities to ensure waterfowl populations are conserved. Many clubs operate unshot refuge areas to provide disturbance free feeding and roosting for birds. Wardens are normally appointed to ensure club rules and codes of practice are upheld. Threats to an estuary's conservation value are also a threat to wildfowlers' sport. Wildfowling management is now used by many, including the government, as an example of how human activity can be integrated with sound wildlife management.

HEDGEROWS

Hedgerows and associated field margins are habitats that provide for a wide range of Britain's plant and animal species. It is estimated that hedgerows extend for some 400,000 km crisscrossing farmland and linking other wildlife habitats. Hedgerows typically consist of shrubs such as hawthorn or blackthorn with hedges of holly, gorse or hazel common in some parts of the country.

A field margin is the outer edge of an arable field which is taken out of cultivation and managed as a grassy strip or wild flower rich area adjacent to a field boundary.

Hedgerows are primarily a man made feature in our landscape and whilst many marked parish boundaries and follow the lines of old woodlands, the majority were planted to make field boundaries or to retain stock.

Overall hedgerows in Britain support 30 species of trees and shrubs and up to 500 species of plants. Many of our familiar songbirds such as robins and blackbirds nest in hedgerows as well as summer visitors such as the whitethroat. Berries provide important food for overwintering species such as redwing and fieldfare. In all, 65 species of birds are dependent in some way on hedgerows. Ditches, which are often found next to hedgerows, and field margins can support reptiles and amphibian species such as newts, toads, frogs and grass snakes which like to bask on sunny hedge banks.

Hedgehogs, shrews and voles are just some of the mammals that spend most of their life in the hedgerow. In areas of the countryside where woodlands or other important habitats are fragmented, hedgerows are invaluable as a corridor of dispersal for many of our mammals, game birds, insects and plants.

About 1,500 insects rely on hedgerows. This includes species such as the bush cricket which are more commonly heard than seen, as well as many butterfly species such as the gatekeeper or hedge brown. Many of our larger butterflies have caterpillars that feed on nettles and thistles growing in the hedge, for example the red admiral, peacock and small tortoiseshell.

Although hedgerows today stretch for some 400,000 km, this represents a 50 per cent reduction from the estimated 800,000 km present at the end of the Second World War. Losses are still taking place at a rate of up to 6,000 km a year. Legislation which came into effect in summer 1997 should go some way to protecting Britain's hedges from being removed.

THE ROLE OF
THE SPORTSMAN

In order to retain their wildlife interest, hedgerows require active management. Today hedgerows are often trimmed mechanically, this can be expensive for the farm and poor practice can damage a wildlife habitat. Different types of hedgerow management in the past created habitats that are now important for our native wildlife. Hedgerows and field margins also provide valuable habitat for game birds such as the pheasant and partridge, and sportsmen have a vested interest in retaining and managing them. The grey partridge prefers nesting in grassy hedge bottoms moving out into field margins as chicks hatch and begin to feed.

The grey partridge is a bird of lowland farmland that has suffered decline over many years associated with changes in farming practice. Research carried out by The Game Conservancy Trust, on habitat management for the grey partridge has led to the development of conservation techniques that are now widely adopted throughout the UK, such as the conservation headland. This involves selective spraying of cereal crop edges to allow broad-leaved arable weeds and the insects that depend on them to thrive. These are an important food source vital for the survival of gamebird chicks and benefit many other wildlife species.

Gamekeepers control pests and predators that can harm ground nesting birds such as the pheasant and partridge. Control, carried out as part of the wise use of the wildlife resource, is carried out those times of year when the problem exists and targeted at those animals or birds causing the problem. Research shows that where this management takes place many other ground nesting species benefit including, for example, the rare stone curlew found in East Anglia.

Adoption of management practices for hedgerows and field margins, essentially for game species, plays an important role in maintaining the wide diversity of wildlife on farmland.

The shooter's choice of shotgun will largely be determined by the kind of quarry to be sought and the likely range at which it will most often be encountered.

SHOTGUNS

DEFINITION OF A
SHOTGUN

The Firearms Act 1968 (as amended) defines a shotgun as. "A smooth bore gun, not being an air rifle or a revolver gun with a barrel not less than 24 inches and with a bore not exceeding 2 inches. It must either have no magazine or a non-detachable magazine incapable of holding more than two cartridges and certified in writing by a proof house or other approved person"

This definition requires further explanation as it allows for a number of variations incorporating a number of different features.

THE COMPONENT PARTS
OF A SHOTGUN

There are various types and styles of shotguns available. The 'standard game gun' is here examined, since it is the type most commonly used.

The traditional game gun

The Traditional game gun is a double-barrel side-by-side hammerless ejector 12-bore shotgun of drop-down opening style. It has a top lever and barrels between 635mm (25in) and 760mm (30in) in length, with either a side or boxlock action, double triggers and an automatic safety catch. It has fairly open choke and is chambered for 65mm (2½in) or 70mm (2¾in) cartridges. It has a stock, fore-end and rib.

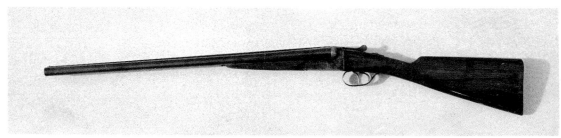

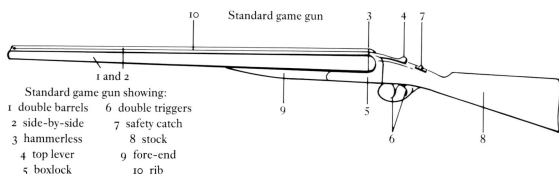

Standard game gun

Standard game gun showing:
1 double barrels   6 double triggers
2 side-by-side   7 safety catch
3 hammerless   8 stock
4 top lever   9 fore-end
5 boxlock   10 rib

You must be able to identify the following components and features of a shotgun:

Double barrel and side-by-side

Double barrel means that the shotgun has two barrels; side-by-side refers to the positioning of those two barrels.

position of barrels:
side-by-side

Over-and-under

Alternatively, the two barrels may be placed one above the other. This style of shotgun is known as an 'over-and-under'. Over and under shotguns are becoming more popular in all areas of shotgun shooting. In some areas they dominate, such as in clay pigeon shooting.

position of barrels:
'over-and-under'

Single and three-barrelled shotguns

The most common alternative to the double-barrel shotgun is the single barrel. Guns have been made which have three barrels, the third usually being placed centrally below the other two in a side-by-side position. In such guns the third barrel is normally rifled (i.e. internally grooved) and is intended for use against large ground game. These guns are more common on the continent than in the United Kingdom. You cannot possess such a gun in the United Kingdom unless you have a Firearms Certificate on which the gun is specified.

The construction of shotgun barrels

Modern shotgun barrels are made of steel and are either drilled or drawn out of a solid cylindrical piece of steel.

Damascus barrels

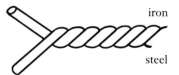

iron

steel

An alternative method of constructing shotgun barrels by twisting thin strands of iron and steel together and welding them into a barrel shape is now obsolete. Barrels made in this manner are known as Damascus barrels; they may be found on a number of guns still in use. Many will not have been proved (see p. 31) for modern nitro powders, and can only be safely used with black powder.

composition of Damascus barrels: the iron and steel strands when welded together will be formed into a barrel shape

Hammerless

Hammerless refers to the absence of visible exterior hammers.

Hammerless guns were first patented in 1863. Hammer guns are still in common use, but a number of older ones may not have been proved (see p. 31) for use with modern cartridges.

hammerless gun
(Anson & Deeley action)

hammer gun

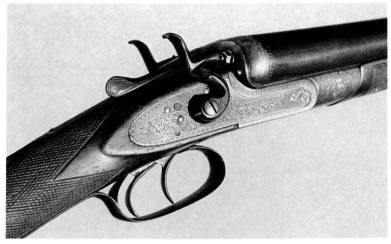

Ejector

The ejector throws out, or ejects, fired cartridges when the gun is opened; non-fired cartridges are not ejected.

The alternative to the ejector is known as the non-ejector. Non-ejectors do not throw out fired cartridges, but will lift empty cases slightly – thus enabling the user to grip the cartridge and manually extract it.

Semi-automatic (see p. 25) and pump-action shotguns (see p. 25) eject as part of the sequence of firing and bringing up the next cartridge into the chamber.

Bore of a shotgun

Shotguns are classified by the size of the bore, which is the internal diameter of the barrel. The bore Size or gauge is measured by the number of perfectly spherical balls of pure lead, each exactly fitting the interior diameter of the barrel, required to make up 1lb in weight.

how a bore is measured:
12-bore

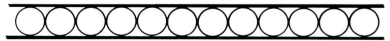

Therefore, because a 20-bore requires 20 such lead spheres, and a 12-bore requires 12, the 20-bore must be of a smaller bore than the 12-bore.

The different bores available are 4, 8, 10, 12, 16, 20 and 28 bore. There is also a .410. The .410 is not measured by the number of spherical lead balls, each exactly fitting the diameter of the barrel, required to make up 1lb (454 grammes) in weight, but refers to the nominal internal diameter of the barrel in inches.

The standard game gun is a 12-bore. The 12-bore is suitable for all types of sporting shotgun shooting provided the appropriate cartridge is used (see. p. 26). however 20 bores are becoming very popular.

The 4, 8 and 10-bore are normally used only for coastal wildfowling, although the 12-bore is perfectly adequate. The 4, 8 and 10-bore are no longer in common use.

The 16-bore is suitable for most forms of inland shooting, but is more commonly used on the Continent than in this country.

The 20-bore is a suitable light-weight game and general purpose inland gun.

The 28-bore and the .410 are normally used to introduce youngsters to shotguns, but their limited range severely limits their value and could discourage youngsters from continuing in the sport. It may be advisable to wait until the beginner is capable of handling a 20 or 12-bore with light cartridge loads.

Drop-down action

Drop-down action refers to the manner in which the shotgun is opened for the purposes of loading and reloading.

drop-down action of a
side-by-side

Other opening styles

Not all shotguns have a drop-down action. On semi-automatic and pump-action shotguns the barrel does not drop down to enable the user to insert a cartridge into the chamber; instead, the cartridge is placed in the chamber as part of the manual or semi-automatic process of firing. On bolt-action shotguns the cartridge is inserted into the chamber which is exposed by pulling the bolt back.

semi-automatic action
(shown open)

bolt-action shotgun

Advantage of the
drop-down action

A distinct advantage of the drop-down style is that it allows the user to easily check that the barrels are clear of an obstruction before loading, or after an obstruction may have entered the muzzle (for example, when shooting in snow or mud, and after any abnormal noise or recoil on firing).

Top lever

The top lever is the manual means by which the standard game gun is opened.

Although the top lever is standard, some guns have an under lever; some have side levers, but these are rare.

Non drop-down guns do not require opening levers.

side lever

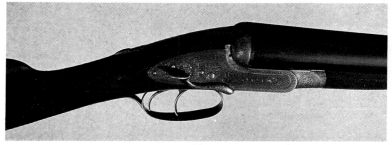

Boxlock and sidelock action

Boxlock and sidelock are the alternative actions to be found in standard game guns. The action is, in simplified terms, the firing mechanism.

Boxlocks are cheaper to manufacture than sidelocks because they are simpler in design and have fewer components.

Sidelock actions are larger and heavier than boxlock actions, but allow for easier access to the mechanism for cleaning.

Triggers

The majority of double-barrel shotguns are fitted with double triggers, one for each barrel.

On a side-by-side with double triggers, the right hand side-trigger fires the right barrel and the left-hand side-trigger fires the left barrel. The right trigger is in front of the left trigger. (This applies to a right-hand gun, which is the manner in which most are manufactured. Left-hand guns are normally only made to specification.)

Double-barrel shotguns can be fitted with a single trigger which may or may not be selective. If the single trigger is selective, the shooter can choose which barrel he fires first, thus allowing for a choice of choke. The selecting device is normally incorporated into the safety catch. The single non-selective trigger will fire the right barrel first and the left barrel second.

On an over-and-under shotgun with double triggers, the right trigger fires the bottom barrel and the left trigger fires the top barrel. However many over-and-unders have a selective trigger.

The Safety Catch

The safety catch bolts the triggers so that they cannot be pulled. This does not mean, however, that the internal hammers are locked: they remain cocked and poised over the cartridges. The gun could be discharged by a knock or a jar, or even a hard pull on the trigger.

A shotgun with cartridges in the chambers is not safe – no matter what postion the safety catch is in.

Automatic safety catches

Safety catches may be: automatic, i.e. returning to safe when the gun is opened.

Non-automatic safety catches

Or: non-automatic, i.e. not returning as part of the process of opening the gun.

Take extra care with safety catches which are non-automatic.

Do not rely on any safety catch to make a shotgun safe

Many semi-automatic pump-action shotguns have a sliding-button safety catch on the side of the action which is usually non-automatic.

See p. 38 for recommendation on the use of the safety catch.

Choke

Choke refers to constriction at the muzzle end of the bore of a shotgun: that is at the end of the barrel which gives a certain amount of inward propulsion to the shot. This is necessary because as soon as the pellets leave the muzzle they begin to spread; the further they travel, the more they spread. Eventually they will spread so much that not enough pellets will hit the target.

Degrees of choke

a degree of choke
at the muzzle

The five degrees of choke are:
  (i) Full choke – tightest degree of restriction
  (ii) Three-quarter choke
  (iii) Half choke
  (iv) Quarter Choke
  (v) One-eighth choke (often referred to as improved cylinder)

True cylinder

Finally, if there is no degree of restriction at the muzzle and the diameter is the same at the muzzle as along the whole bore this is known as true cylinder.

Effect of choke

Pattern is the distribution of pellets in a given circle at a given range; the tightest pattern, i.e. the greatest number of pellets in that circle, is produced by full choke and the most open by the true cylinder.

pattern produced by true cylinder (*top*)
and full choke (*bottom*)

A standard load 12-bore cartridge will place the following number of pellets in a 760mm (30in) circle at a range of 35m (about 40yd):

Degree of Choke	Percentage of Pellets ex 300		
Full	225		75%
Three-quarter	195		65%
Half	180	in a 760mm (30in circle)	60%
Quarter	150	at 35m (about 40yd)	50%
Improved cylinder	135		45%
True cylinder	120		40%

From the foregoing it might be assumed that the degree of choke which places the greatest number of pellets onto the target is the most desirable and that full choke would be most suitable. This would be true if all shots fired were accurately aimed and if all shots were taken at 35m (about 40yd) range. In Britain most shooting is at targets much less than 35m (about 40yd) away. Few trees exceed 14m (15yd) in height and most inland shooting occurs at about tree-top height.

The degree of choke used is largely dependent upon personal choice; but many, if not most, people use more open than tight chokes, often with improved cylinder in the right barrel and quarter or half choke in the left.

Removal of choke	**Choke can be removed, but it cannot be replaced.** The only exception is recess choke where it can be replaced to a certain extent. Most guns are fitted with normal and not recess choke.
Recess choke	Recess choke is usually found in top-class shotguns. On a standard side-by-side game gun the right barrel has a more open choke than the top barrel. On over-and-under shotguns the lower barrel usually has a more open choke than the left. Single-barrel shotguns are limited to one choke (unless fitted with one of the proprietary brands of variable choke devices which are now available).
Multi choke	Many guns are now available with interchangeable chokes that vary in their degree of restriction. These enable the shooter to vary the pellet pattern. They need to be kept clean and seated carefully otherwise the barrels may become damaged.
Tight choke	**A tight choke does not increase the range of a shotgun (see p.27).**
Chambers	The chamber of a shotgun is that part of the barrel nearest to the action into which the cartridge is inserted. Most 12-bore shotguns are chambered for 65mm (2½in), 70mm (2¾in) or 75mm (3 in) cartridges. **It is potentially dangerous to fire any cartridge in a gun designed for a smaller cartridge – i.e. with a smaller chamber length**
Stock	The stock has two functions: one is to house part of the action; the other is to ensure that the shotgun when brought up to the shoulder is correctly aligned with the shooter's 'master' eye.
Master eye	Everybody has a master eye: the 'master' eye looks directly at objects. It is essential that you shoot from the same shoulder as your master eye. If you have a right master eye, shoot from the right shoulder and if you have a left master eye, shoot from the left shoulder. To determine which is your 'master' eye follow this simple procedure: 1 Hold a pencil upright at arm's length in your left hand. 2 Look through both eyes and line the pencil point up with an object on the other side of the room (for example, a light switch). 3 Place your right hand over your right eye. If the pencil and the object are no longer in line, you have a right master eye. 4 Place your right hand over your left eye. The object will still be in line with the pencil. If, when you placed your right hand over the right eye, the object and the pencil were still in line, then you have a left master eye. Shotgun stocks are traditionally made of walnut which can be bent or cast to suit the shooter's requirements. However modern materials such as plastic are becoming more common.

A stock is measured as shown in the illustration below:

how a stock is measured:
A bend to comb
B bend to heel
C length to heel
D length to butt
E length to toe

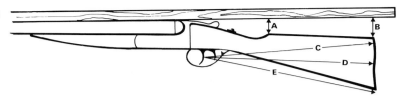

'Cast' of a stock

The term 'cast' refers to the degree to which the stock is bent out of straight in relation to the line of the barrel(s) in order to bring the barrel(s) in line with the user's master eye.

Cast is measured at the butt and is termed 'cast off' if it is to the right and 'cast on' if it is to the left.

Shapes of shotgun stocks

The standard game gun usually has a 'straight' stock. This enables the user to manipulate the rear trigger. Single-trigger shotguns are normally fitted with a pistol or semi-pistol grip.

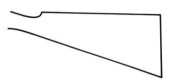  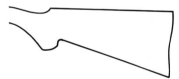

different stocks: straight (*left*) semi-pistol (*middle*) full pistol (*right*)

The fore-end

One of the functions of the fore-end is that it provides the forward grip for the shooter. It should not be too smooth and it should be large enough to prevent the fingers of the forward hand encroaching upon the rib and thus obstructing the line of sight.

Most standard game guns are fitted with a narrow fore-end, known as an English fore-end; a common variant is the broad American style beaver-tail fore-end. Choice is largely dependent upon personal preferences. The fore-end also serves to lock the barrels into position.

English fore-end

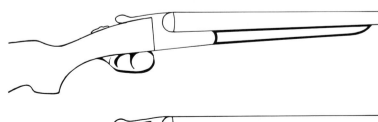

American beaver-tail fore-end

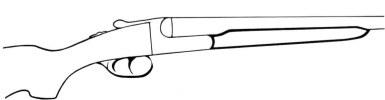

The rib	On a side-by-side shotgun the rib is used to secure the barrels to each other and as a sighting device along which to line up the barrels on to the target.
	On over-and-under shotguns, the rib is used solely as a sighting plane.
PUMP–ACTION AND SEMI-AUTOMATIC SHOTGUNS	Pump-action and semi-automatic shotguns can be operated on one of three principles: manual, gas pressure or recoil.
	The Firearms (Amendment) Act 1988 now classifies any of the above guns with a magazine capacity of more than two cartridges as a Section 1 Firearm requiring a Firearm Certificate. For them to be treated in law as shotguns they should have a non-detachable magazine incapable of holding more than two cartridges and be certified in writing by a proof house or other approved person. It is important to retain the proof house certificate with the gun.
Pump action:	Manually operated pump-action shotguns have a sliding fore-end which, when pulled back and pushed forward, ejects the fired cartridge and brings the next cartridge from the magazine into the chamber, ready for firing.
Gas operated self-loading shotguns	Gas pressure-operated self-loaders work by an impulsion of the propellant gas into a cylinder which operates a mechanism in the breech which will eject the fired cartridge.
Recoil operated self-loading shotguns:	Recoil operated semi-automatic shotguns work by a process of barrel or chamber recoil generated by the shot. The principle remains the same as for the manually operated pump-action shotgun except that the 'pump' occurs automatically on recoil.
Side-by-side and self-loading shotguns	**The standard side-by-side shotgun has stood the test of time and is universally accepted whereas pump-action and self-loaders shotguns are not always welcomed on formal driven shoots (see Chapter 8). This is largely because it is not possible to see whether these guns are empty, as it is with a double barrelled gun when 'broken', or open. However there is nothing inherently dangerous about pump action or self-loading shotguns.**

SHOTGUN CARTRIDGES

Production of a shotgun certificate (see Chapter 4) is necessary to purchase ammunition unless the purchaser shows he is exempt from the need for a certificate. Ammunition can be purchased for someone else if you possess their certificate and written authority.

As with shotguns, the shotgun cartridge will be examined by discussing the standard 12-bore game cartridge and the variations available.

THE STRUCTURE OF A SHOTGUN CARTRIDGE

One of the most commonly used 12-bore cartridges is 65mm (2½in) in length, has a case which is made of plastic and which is crimp closed and throws a load of 28g. (1oz.) of shot.

THE COMPONENT PARTS AND FEATURES OF A SHOTGUN CARTRIDGE AND THEIR FUNCTIONS

composition of standard game cartridge

1 case
2 wad
3 powder
4 crimp closure
5 shot (load)
6 primer

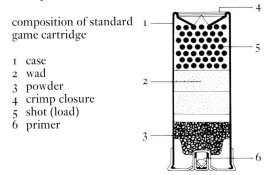

The length of the cartridge

A 65mm (2½in) cartridge is suitable for use in a 70mm (2¾in) chamber gun. Cartridges which are longer than the chamber length of the gun should not be used.

The cartridge case

The case is the outer shell of the cartridge. It has three functions: it is a container for the remaining components of the cartridge; it has to retain the shot until the correct moment and it has to seal the chamber so that all the pressure is directed down the barrel and is not allowed to escape.

It is preferable that the case is waterproof and for this reason cartridges are now commonly manufactured with plastic or polyethylene cases.

Cartridges were previously manufactured with paper cases; the main disadvantages with paper cases are that they are not waterproof and may warp if they become damp. Paper cases may also split if they become abnormally dry.

Store paper cases at normal room temperature, out of the sun and away from sources of heat and damp.

An advantage of paper-cased cartridges is that the case disintegrates if left on the ground. Plastic cases do not. The most sensible approach is to pick up all empty cartridge cases and not to leave litter.

Crimp closures

Crimp closure refers to the manner in which the cartridge is sealed in order to retain its components. The case is made sufficiently long to allow the top to be turned in towards the centre in a star pattern.

Roll closures

The alternative method is roll closure. The end of the cartridge is pressed over a wad which retains the components.

| *The Load* | Shot is small balls of lead of various sizes. In descending order from single to dust shot, The sizes are given specific names: |

Single
L.G.
S.G
Sp. S.G.
S.S.G.
A.A.A.
B.B.
1,2,3,4,5,6,7,8, and 9.

and each corresponds to a fixed diameter e.g.

BB = 4.1mm, 6 = 2.6mm although sizes can vary in different countries

The total weight of shot in cartridge is the *load* and this varies according to the type of shooting, for example 24, 28, 30, and 32 grammes etc.

Replacement of lead shot

From September 1999 the Government prohibited the use of lead shot over all foreshore, many wetland Sites of Special Scientific interest (S.S.S.I.) and for shooting all waterfowl. Steel, bismuth, tin, tungsten and a few other materials have been developed and are being used in place of lead. Their characteristics are different from lead and different loads, shot sizes, components and shooting techniques may be needed. For up-to-date information contact BASC.

Recommended shot sizes

The following shot sizes are normally recommended in a standard 12-bore game gun for the following species:

Partridge 6/7	Pheasant 5/6/7	Snipe 8
Grouse 6/7	Woodcock 7	Geese BB/1/3
Pigeon 6/7	Teal 6/7	Mallard 4/5/6
Hare 4/5	Rabbit 5/6	Squirrel 7

The standard game load is 30g (1¹/₁₆oz) of number 6 shot, although many game shooters will use either No 5 or No 7 shot. Please note some lead free shot is less dense than lead and may necessitate going up one or two sizes in shot size. Steel is an example of one such material.

The loads may range from the 51g. (2oz) in the 4-bore used for wildfowling to the smaller loads used in the .410 such as the 8g. (⁵/₁₆ oz) load.

A heavier load does not increase the effective range of a shotgun.

Shotgun range

The range of a shotgun is not simply the maximum range at which a shotgun is capable of killing a particular quarry. This would mean that a shotgun or cartridge combination

which was capable of killing by hitting a vital spot on the target occasionally could result in a large number of instances of wounding without killing.

In order to define the range of a shotgun we can do no better than to quote Gough Thomas from his book *Shotguns and Cartridges for Game and Clays* in which he states: '. . . the maximum effective range of a gun in relation to a given kind of game is the greatest range at which it is reasonably certain that a clean kill will be made by a truly aimed shot.'

In effect, this means that with a standard load 12-bore cartridge the maximum effective range will be 32–37m (35– 40yd).

Smaller bore guns will have a correspondingly lower maximum effective range. All bores create similar patterns, but in the smaller bore guns the effect of this will be to reduce the number of pellets in the target .

THE CARE AND MAINTENANCE OF A SHOTGUN

There are three good reasons for maintaining a shotgun in good working order: (*i*) to ensure that it remains in a safe condition; (*ii*) to reduce the risk of mechanical malfunction at any time; (*iii*) to preserve an asset which may appreciate if well looked after.

There are a number of methods and materials which may be used. The following is one method which will enable a shotgun to be kept clean and rust free.

The recommended cleaning kit consists of:

a cleaning rod
tissue paper, kitchen paper or rolled-up newspaper
a proprietary brand of gun cleaner – in either oil or spray form
a phosphor bronze brush
a lambswool mop
pipe-cleaners
a soft cloth/rag

The following recommendations are based on the assumption that the shotgun has been fired on a particularly wet day.

First detach the barrels from the stock

TO CLEAN THE STOCK

Hold the stock firmly and give it a good shake. On a wet day water which has penetrated the mechanism will thus be shaken out.

Remove all visible water from the exterior of the stock.

Remove any mud, dirt or blood from the stock and clean the chequering, possibly with a soft toothbrush, to remove any dirt.

Rub over the mechanism with an oily rag.

TO CLEAN THE FORE-END   Use the same method as for the stock.

TO CLEAN THE BARRELS   Remove all visible water from the barrels and run a piece of tissue, as tightly as possible, along the guttering beside the rib.

Fold or roll-up the newspaper or tissue and push it through the barrels with the cleaning rod – the tissue should be as tight as possible – from the chamber to the muzzle. This will remove the worst of the fouling and will enable you to keep your cleaning materials relatively clean.

The next stage is to attach the phosphor bronze brush to the cleaning rod and with short, sharp backward-and-forward movements work the brush all the way along the inside of the barrels to remove all traces of lead residue.

The barrels, when held up to a light and looked through, should be bright with no tell-tale streaks visible. To complete this stage of the cleaning, put a thin smear of oil along the inside of the barrels using the lambswool mop or spray. Remember that the oil must be removed before the gun is used again.

Raise the extractors and with a pipe-cleaner, or a piece of cloth over a small stick, clean out any remaining powder residues.

GENERAL MAINTENANCE   Below are some general points that you should also be aware of:

Do not 'over oil' a shotgun, as this can result in a 'gumming-up' of the moving parts. The parts which require the merest drop of oil from time to time are those which recieve the greatest friction. On a sidelock-action it is a straightforward process to remove the locks to enable drying and cleaning of the action. With a boxlock it involves the removal of the bottom plate (positioned just forward of the trigger guard).

Whenever attempting to remove any screw, it is essential that the screwdriver is of an accurate fit to avoid damaging the screw.

If your gun has received an extensive soaking, place it in a warm, dry area with the barrels in such a position as to allow any water which has remained in the gutters alongside the rib to run off. Do not place the stock too near a direct source of heat or in too warm a place, as the wood may warp or split. Re-examine the gun the following day to make doubly sure that no rust has begun to accumulate.

When cleaning your gun, examine it for faults and/or damage.

If you are not using your gun for some time, then examine it frequently to ensure that no rust is buliding up while it is in storage.

When putting your gun into its case, or slip, hold the barrels with a cloth to avoid leaving sweat marks which could form the basis for rust.

Shotguns should be sent to a competent gunsmith for a clean and overhaul every year. Do this well before the season opens in order to avoid a last minute panic.

3   Shotgun Safety

Always check that a shotgun is unloaded immediately you handle it.

It is not sufficient simply to believe that a shotgun is unloaded when you first handle it; it must be an automatic reaction to check that it is unloaded by opening it, if it is of the drop-down variety, or by examining the breech and chamber, if it is a pump or self-loading action gun.

Accidents have occurred when a gun was believed to be empty.

You must check.

checking that a shotgun is unloaded (*left*)

passing a shotgun stock first with the breach open and empty (*below*)

Always pass a shotgun to someone stock first with the breech open and empty.

Always treat any gun as loaded and therefore potentially dangerous.

Always ensure that the barrels are not pointed at anything which you do not intend to shoot.

Always carry a shotgun open and empty when in company.

Even when you have emptied the gun or checked that it is unloaded, do not assume that safety precautions can be disregarded.

Always take special care with pump-action and self-loading guns.

In close company carry such guns with the slide or action open and with the muzzle pointing upwards.

With pump-action or self-loading shotguns always take special care to ensure that there is no obstruction in the barrel.

Always ensure that any shotgun you intend to use is in a safe and sound condition.

Make certain that the internal mechanism is in a proper state of adjustment.

You must be able to recognise the following potential problems which can occur with shotguns:

Denting and/or bulging of the barrel

A dent causes a restriction in the barrel which will result in excessive pressure in the barrel. A bulge is a weakening of the structure of the barrel.

Pitting of the barrels

Pitting can occur both inside and outside barrel bores and will result in a weakening of the barrel strength. It is caused by poor care and maintenance.

Raised ribs

Raised ribs will involve a weakening of the barrel wall (if caused by rusting) and almost certainly a weakening of the barrel structure.

Damaged or cracked stocks

A cracked stock may break as a result of recoil and is a potential hazard to the shooter and anyone nearby.

A loose action

The action should be correctly aligned to the barrels to ensure that pressure is not allowed to escape when the gun is fired.

Always have your gun regularly overhauled by a competent gunsmith.

Have faults rectified immediately. A gun should be annually inspected by a gunsmith.

Always ensure that you understand the proof markings on any shotgun you use.

The law relating to the proofing of guns is to be found in the Gun Barrel Proof Acts 1868, 1950 and 1978 and in various Rules of Proof. Whilst the Acts and Rules are complex, the reason for the need to understand the proof markings on any gun you use is straightforward.

The proof marks will show whether or not a gun has been tested for particular loads and powders.

Cartridges with a heavier load than that

indicated by the proof mark should not be used.

The proof marks and explanatory notes appear in Appendix 3.

Always ensure that any gun you intend to use is safe and in proof for the cartridge you intend to use.

If any doubt exists, the gun should be examined by a gunsmith because:
1. **An unproofed gun will be in a dangerous condition and should not be used. It is a hazard not only to the user but to any other person nearby.**
2. **It is illegal to sell or offer for sale an unproofed gun. The maximum penalty is £1,000 for each offence.**

Always remember that a shotgun may be out of proof.

Always remember that there are particular problems relating to hammer guns.

Always carry hammer guns in the uncocked position, with the hammers down.

Upon the immediate expectation of a shot, cock the hammers whilst ensuring that the barrels are pointing straight upwards, placing the fingers around the outside of the trigger guard and the thumb in the crutch of the hammer.

Always open the gun before uncocking the hammers.

If you cock the hammers in the expectation of a shot but do not fire them, do not uncock the hammers onto loaded chambers.

If the right hammer in the cocked position obstructs the top lever, consult a gunsmith.

Always leave a shotgun in such a way that it cannot be knocked over or fall.

The barrels of a shotgun are made of steel, but they can easily be damaged by a knock or fall. If you must put an unloaded shotgun down, pay particular attention to where it is placed, avoiding all hazards.

Never put a loaded shotgun down.

Never mix cartridges for shotguns of different bores.

If, for example, a 20-bore cartridge is placed into the chamber of a 12-bore, it will enter the barrel far enough to allow a 12-bore cartridge to be placed above it and the gun to be closed and fired. The result will almost certainly be serious damage to the gun which may cause injury or death.

Never allow unsupervised children to handle guns or cartridges.

Children are by nature inquisitive and want to find out about things, guns and cartridges being no exception, so lock guns and cartridges away out of reach.

Introduce youngsters to supervised correct gun-handling at an appropriate age.

SHOTGUN SAFETY IN THE HOME

Never load a shotgun indoors

This rule is absolute. There is no reason whatsoever for loading a shotgun indoors.

Always store your shotgun and cartridges securely.

Always keep your shotguns and cartridges in separate, safe places, locked away, out of sight.

Since the Firearms (Amendment) Act 1988 it is necessary to keep shotguns in a secure place when not in actual use. The definition of a secure place is not made clear and before spending money on security it is advisable to consult your local Crime Prevention Officer for advice.

Always keep a record of shotgun serial numbers or, if there is no number, of any other distinguishing marks.

In the event of loss or theft of your shotgun this will enable you to give a full and accurate description to the police; a photograph is ideal. See notes on shotgun certificate content (page 41).

SHOTGUN SAFETY WHILST TRAVELLING

Never travel with a loaded shotgun

Before entering a vehicle check that your shotgun is unloaded. When anyone enters a vehicle with a shotgun which is not in a case or cover or you cannot see that it is empty, satisfy yourself that the gun is unloaded.

Always when travelling carry your shotgun in a case or a protective cover.

This will serve to protect the gun against any possible damage.

Always when travelling to or from a shoot ensure that your shotgun and cartridges are stored out of sight in the vehicle.

This helps to safeguard your property.

Always lock unattended vehicles.

Whenever leaving a vehicle which contains guns or cartridges, even if only for a very brief period, make certain that the vehicle is securely locked. Try to remove a component from the gun and carry it with you where possible.

Always carry a shotgun so that it cannot point at anyone, always be muzzle aware.

how to carry a gun over the crook of the elbow

Always unload your shotgun before crossing an obstacle, or negotiating difficult terrain. In company, you must:

1. Open your shotguns. 2. Remove cartridges. 3. One shooter passes his gun, open and stock first, to his companion. 4–5. Having crossed the obstacle, the shooter takes both guns from his companion. 6. The second shooter crosses the obstacle. 7. He takes back his gun.

If a shooting companion attempts to cross an obstacle without following this procedure, politely but firmly insist that he does.

how to cross an obstacle with a companion (1–7)

 2

 3

 4

 5

 6

 7

how to cross an obstacle alone (1–5)

Procedure when alone

Do not attempt to negotiate an obstacle without removing the cartridges from the shotgun chamber.

If possible lay the gun down, cross the obstacle and pick the gun up.

These procedures apply to fences, gates, hedges, ditches, steep banks, fallen trees, etc.

Always look through your barrels to check whenever an obstruction could have entered.

Always be certain that the gun is proofed for the cartridges you intend to use.

Always be aware of the possibility, and the consequences, of a misfire, which is when a cartridge refuses to fire. You should also beware of a hangfire. In this situation the cartridge does fire, but only after a delay, which could be as long as 30 seconds.

Always load a shogun by placing the cartridge in the chamber and raising the stock to the barrel.

Always make sure the barrels are pointing in a safe direction when reloading.

Always keep your fingers well clear of the triggers except when taking a shot.

If there is an uncharacteristic noise or recoil from a particular shot, make certain that you look down the barrel in a safe fashion, before taking another shot to determine that there is no obstruction.

Always be certain of your 'Safe Arc of Fire'.

See p. 27 for an explanation of maximum effective range.

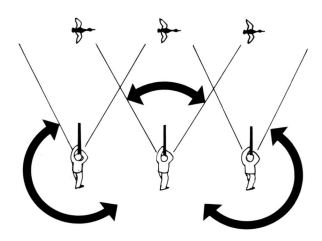

safe arc of fire

Always be aware of what is beyond your target.

Do not fire if you cannot see where the shot will go: i.e. at bushes or at a hedge. Do not fire where ricochets could occur: i.e. at rocks or water.

Details of safety procedures to be adopted whilst engaging in various aspects of the sport are discussed further in Chapter 7 (pp. 104–5) and Chapter 8 (pp. 110–111).

Always be sure of what you are shooting.

Positively identify your target before raising your shotgun to the shooting position. If in doubt – do not shoot.

SAFETY CATCHES
Always have the safety catch on 'safe' until the moment before you wish to fire.

The safety catch should not be released until the gun is mounted to the shoulder.

Always put the safety catch back on between shots. Take special care with guns without automatic safety catches.

Do no unnecessarily push the safety catch on and off whilst awaiting a shot.

The term safety catch is misleading as it does not mean that a gun cannot be fired. A mechanical device can be defective. Use the safety catch as recommended, but never handle a shotgun believing that the safety catch will stop it discharging.

how to close a shotgun

Never load a shotgun until you are about to start shooting.

Never attempt to shoot unless you are steady on your feet.

A shot taken whilst unsteady could result in the shooter losing balance at the moment of firing.

Never attach a dog's lead to yourself, whilst shooting.

If the dog is unsteady enough to require to be tied up, it may decide to move as you are about to fire, thus causing you to over-balance.

Never shoot without public Liability insurance.

Membership of BASC provides public liabilty insurance up to £5 million.

Safety is a level of consciousness – not a fortunate series of events

---

Safety is the responsibility of everyone – including you.

4 The Law Relating to Shooting

The Firearms (Amendment) Act 1988 brought in stricter controls particularly in relation to the ownership of shotguns.

SHOTGUN CERTIFICATES IN ENGLAND, WALES AND SCOTLAND

THE SHOTGUN CERTIFICATE
If you wish to purchase or own a shotgun, as defined in Chapter 2, you must possess a valid shotgun certificate.

The Firearms Acts 1968–1994 apply.

Transfer of shotguns

It is illegal (subject to limited exceptions) to buy or sell a shotgun unless both the vendor and the purchaser hold valid shotgun certificates.

When a shotgun is transferred to anyone other than a Registered Firearms Dealer each party to the transaction must notify his own Chief Officer of Police within seven days by either registered post or recorded delivery. "Transfer" includes selling, giving as a gift, hiring or a loan of over seventy-two hours.

HOW TO OBTAIN A SHOTGUN CERTIFICATE

Obtain an application form from the police. Complete it and have it countersigned as described on the form.

Unless the police tell you otherwise, you should then take or send it with the appropriate fee to your local police station.

Shotgun certificates are valid for FIVE years from the date of issue. Certain constabularies may issue reminders to shotgun certificate holders shortly before the expiry date of the certificate.

In any event, it is the shotgun certificate holder's own responsibility to renew his certificate.

A shotgun certificate will specify the descriptions of the shotguns to which it relates. This will include, where known, the identification numbers of the guns. The new shotgun certificates will have a statutory safe keeping requirement, and a requirement to notify the police of any change of address.

CONDITIONS OF ISSUE

A shotgun certificate is issued subject to the following conditions:
1. The holder must, on receipt of the certificate, sign it in ink with his usual signature.
2. The holder of a shotgun certificate must immediately inform the Chief Officer of the police force by whom it was granted of the theft or loss in Great Britain of any shotgun in his possession.
3. The police may refuse to issue a shotgun certificate if they are satisfied that an applicant does not have a good reason for possessing the gun, or cannot be permitted to possess a shotgun without danger to public safety or the peace.

THEFT OR LOSS OF A SHOTGUN CERTIFICATE

Since it is illegal to possess a shotgun unless you hold a certificate, you must immediately inform the Chief Officer of the police force by whom it was granted if you lose your shotgun certificate or have it stolen. If you do not do so you may be guilty of an offence.

Although it is not a condition of issue, it is stated on the shotgun certificate that you should notify the Chief Officer of the police force which issued the certificate of any change of address, and send your certificate for replacement.

Failure to do so may lead to delay in renewal.

EXEMPTIONS FROM REQUIREMENT FOR A SHOTGUN CERTIFICATE

As stated above, certain categories of persons do not require a shotgun certificate. These are:
1. A person carrying a firearm (including shotgun) or ammunition belonging to another person holding a certificate under the Firearms Act 1968 may, without himself holding such a certificate, have in his possession that firearm or ammunition under instructions from that other person and for the use of that other person for sporting purposes only.

This may be interpreted to include for example a loader.
2. A person may, without holding a shotgun certificate, borrow a shotgun from the occupier of private premises (including private land) and use it on those premises in the occupier's presence.
3. A person may, without holding a shotgun certificate, use a shotgun at a time and place approved for shooting at artificial targets by the Chief Officer of the police force for the area in which that place is situated.

This may be interpreted to include a shooting school or clay-pigeon shooting ground.

4. Visitors who wish to use, possess, purchase or acquire shotguns and ammunition in Great Britain must obtain a visitor's shotgun permit. The application for such permits must be made on the applicant's behalf by a "sponsoring person" resident in Great Britain and is administered by the Chief Officer of Police for the area in which the sponsoring person resides.

5. A person does not commit an offence if he has in his possession, purchases, or acquires a shotgun if he holds a firearms certificate issued in Northern Ireland authorising him to possess a shotgun (see below).

In addition to the Visitor's Permit, the European Firearms Pass (EFP) is required for those residing in the EU. These will be obtained from country of origin. Certificate holders in UK can obtain a EFP from their constabulary licensing department, free of charge, on request at issue, renewal or any time in between. The EFP is valid for the life of your certificate and is renewable but remains free of charge. Bear in mind that changes to your certificate(s) should also be applied to your EFP. (This applied to both Shotgun and Firearm Certificate holders.)

FIREARMS CERTIFICATES IN NORTHERN IRELAND

REQUIREMENT FOR A CERTIFICATE

Under the Firearms (Northern Ireland) Order 1981, if you wish to have in your possession, purchase, or acquire a shotgun you must obtain authorisation from the Chief Constable, Royal Ulster Constabulary, Brooklyn, Knock Road, Belfast BT5 6LE.

There is no distinction bewteen shotgun, or rifle in Northern Ireland. Certification is dealt with on a single form, regulated and controlled by the R.U.C. The authorised possession of a Northern Ireland firearms certificate exempts the holder from holding a shotgun certificate in England, Scotland and Wales.

EXEMPTION FROM REQUIREMENT FOR FIREARMS CERTIFICATE IN NORTHERN IRELAND

It is not an offence under the Order for any person to have in his possession a firearm (including a shotgun) or ammunition if he can show that by virtue of the Order he is entitled to have possession of the firearm without holding a certificate.

For example: Section 12 (1) permits a person to carry a firearm or ammunition belonging to another person holding a firearms certificate, without himself holding such a certificate, and to have in his possession that firearm or ammunition under instructions from and for the use of that other person for sporting purposes only.

Persons holding valid certificates granted in Great Britain will be exempt from acquiring the equivalent certificate in Northern Ireland, (Section 15.)

THE ACQUISITION AND POSSESSION OF
SHOTGUNS BY PERSONS UNDER THE AGE OF 18

THE PURCHASE, POSSESSION AND USE OF SHOTGUNS BY JUNIORS IN ENGLAND, SCOTLAND AND WALES

There is no lower age limit for possession of a shotgun certificate, but there are limitations on the age at which juniors may possess or purchase shotguns and ammunition.

UNDER 15 YEARS OLD

It is an offence to make a gift of a shotgun or ammunition to a person under 15 years old.

A person under 15 may not have an assembled shotgun with him except:
(i) when he is under the direct supervision of someone of or over 21, in which case he may use the shotgun, providing he has a valid shotgun certificate, under that person's instructions;
(ii) when the shotgun is in a securely fastened gun cover so that it cannot be fired.

AGED 15–17

A person between 15 and 17 years old may be given or lent a shotgun and ammunition, but he may not buy them.

After reaching the age of 15, a person may use a shotgun without supervision providing he holds a valid shotgun certificate.

AGE 17

On reaching the age of 17 a person may purchase a shotgun providing he holds a valid shotgun certificate, and he may buy ammunition.

JUNIORS IN NORTHERN IRELAND

Subject to the exceptions listed below, a person who being under the age of eighteen years, purchases, acquires or has in his possession a firearm or ammunition shall be guilty of an offence. (Firearms (N.I.) Order 1981. Section 26 (1).)

It is not an offence for any person not being under the age of 16 years old
(a) to have with him a firearm (including a shotgun) or ammunition for sporting purposes when he is in the company, and under the supervision of another person not under the age of 18 who holds a firearms certificate in respect of that firearm or ammunition;
(b) to purchase, acquire or have in his possession a shotgun, or any other firearm of a calibre not exceeding .22in, and ammunition therefore for the purpose of destroying or controlling animals and birds:
(i) on agricultural lands occupied by him;
(ii) on agricultural lands on which he works and on which he also resides.

POLICE POWERS

When out shooting, carry your shotgun certificate with you. A constable may demand from any person whom he believes to be in possession of a shotgun, the production of his shotgun certificate.

If a person upon whom a demand is made fails to produce the certificate or to permit the constable to read it, or to show that he is entitled by virtue of the Act to have the shotgun in his possession without holding a certificate, the constable may seize and detain the shotgun and may require the person to declare to him immediately his name and address.

If under this section of the Firearms Act a person is required to give his name and address to a constable, it is an offence for him to refuse to declare it or to fail to give his true name and address.

APPEALS AGAINST POLICE
DECISION TO REFUSE TO
ISSUE OR RENEW A
SHOTGUN CERTIFICATE

ENGLAND AND WALES

If the police refuse to grant, vary or renew your shotgun certificate, you may appeal to the Crown Court on giving notice within twenty-one days of the refusal to the clerk of the court and the Chief Officer of the police force for the area.

SCOTLAND

In Scotland you may appeal to the Sheriff.

NORTHERN IRELAND

In Northern Ireland you may appeal to the Secretary of State.

SHOTGUNS IN PUBLIC PLACES

CARRYING FIREARM
IN A PUBLIC PLACE

A person commits an offence if, without lawful authority or reasonable excuse (the proof whereof lies on him), he has with him in a public place a loaded shotgun.

Public place includes any highway or any other premises or place to which the public has access at the time in question.

TRESPASSING
WITH FIREARM

A person commits an offence if, while he has a firearm (this includes a shotgun) with him, he enters or is on any land as a trespasser and without reasonable excuse (the proof whereof lies on him). Land includes land covered by water.

A person commits an offence if, while he has a firearm (this includes a shotgun) with him, he enters or is in any building or part of a building as a trespasser and without reasonable excuse (the proof whereof lies on him).

| SHOOTING ON OR NEAR A HIGHWAY | **It is an offence without lawful authority or reasonable excuse to shoot within fifty feet of the centre of a highway if in consequence someone on the highway is injured, interrupted or endangered.** |

| FOOTPATHS AND BRIDLEWAYS | A person having the right to shoot on land over which a right of way (footpath or bridleway) passes has lawful authority and reasonable excuse to have a loaded shotgun on or near the footpath or bridleway. |

THE USE OF SHOTGUNS IN RELATION TO THE WILDLIFE AND COUNTRYSIDE ACT 1981

| THE PROTECTION OF WILD BIRDS | The Wildlife and Countryside Act 1981 protects all wild birds (except those covered by the Game Acts), their nests and eggs, subject to clearly defined exceptions.

These exceptions provide for open seasons during which certain species may be shot, and they lift restrictions on shooting certain 'pests' species throughout the year.

Remember that all species are protected: some receive special protection all year or during the close season.

Penalties for killing or harming otherwise protected species are severe. |

| THE QUARRY SPECIES | The species which may be shot during the open season (see below for details of the seasons) are listed in Schedule 2 Part I in Appendix 4.

The species which are commonly regarded as 'pest species' and which may be shot by 'authorised persons' (see below) throughout the year are listed in Schedule 2 Part II in Appendix 4. |

| AUTHORISED PERSONS | Under the Wildlife and Countryside Act, 'authorised persons' means:
(*a*) the owner or occupier, or and person authorised by the owner or occupier, of the land on which the action authorised is taken;
(*b*) any person authorised in writing by the local authority for the area within which the action authorised is taken;
(*c*) any person authorised in writing by the relevant government conservation body, a water authority, or local fisheries committee constituted under the Sea Fisheries Regulations Act 1966;
but with the proviso that the authorisation of any person for the purpose of this definition shall confer any right of entry upon any land. |

| RACING PIGEONS | **Racing pigeons are not listed in the Schedules, but may not be shot or taken at any time.** |

THE OPEN SEASONS

The seasons during which certain birds may be killed or taken are as follows:

Capercaillie and (except in Scotland)
    Woodcock: 1 October–31 January (inclusive)
Woodcock in Scotland: 1 September–31 January (inc)
Snipe, Common: 12 August–31 January (inc)
Wild Duck and Geese inland: 1 September–31 January (inc)
  on the foreshore: 1 September–20 February (inc)
Other species in Schedule 2 Part I
  (Coot, Moorhen):   1 September–31 January (inc)

It is illegal to shoot Schedule 2 birds on Christmas Day in England, Scotland and Wales, and on Sundays in Scotland and certain counties in England and Wales. (These are listed on p. 116).

The seasons for game birds appear on page 49.

PERIODS OF SPECIAL PROTECTION

Under exceptional circumstances, for example prolonged severe weather or serious pollution, the Secretary of State may protect by order any species of wild bird included in Schedule 1 Part II or Schedule 2 Part I for periods of not more than fourteen days. He will act in accordance with criteria and procedures previously agreed by Government, sporting and conservation organisations. Before making such an order, the Secretary of State shall consult a person appearing to him to be a representative of persons interested in the shooting of birds of the kind proposed to be protected by the order.

RESTRICTED USE OF LEAD SHOT

From September 1999 the Government prohibited the use of lead shot over all foreshore, many wetland Sites of Special Scientific interest (S.S.S.I.) and for shooting of all waterfowl. Steel, bismuth, tin, tungsten and a few other materials have been developed and are being used in place of lead.

PROHIBITED METHODS OF TAKING/KILLING WILD BIRDS, INCLUDING GAME

The following methods (relating to the use of shotguns) of killing or taking wild birds, are prohibited:

1. By using any self-loading shotgun which has a magazine capable of holding more than two cartridges.

2. Any shotgun of which the barrel has an internal diameter at the muzzle of more than 44mm (1¾ inches).

3. The use of any device for illuminating a target.

4. The use of any form of artificial lighting or any mirror or other dazzling device.

5. The use as a decoy of any sound recording, or any live bird, or animal which is tethered, or which is secured by means of braces or other similar appliances, or which is blind, maimed or injured.

6. **The use of mechanically propelled vehicle in immedi-**

ate pursuit of a wild bird for the purpose of killing or taking that bird.

KILLING CERTAIN SPECIES CAUSING DAMAGE

The Act makes provision for an authorised person to shoot any wild bird (other than the species in Schedule 1 – see Appendix 4) if he can show that his action was necessary for preventing serious damage to crops, livestock or fisheries.

Otherwise, the shooting of certain other species which may cause damage is controlled under licence.

BASC will provide information on licence arrangements on request.

THE SALE OF DEAD WILD BIRDS

Generally the sale of dead wild birds is prohibited, but the sale of the following species (Schedule 3 Part II) is allowed at all times:
Pigeon, Feral   Woodpigeon

The sale of the following dead wild birds (Schedule 3 Part III) is allowed during the period 1 September–28 February only:

Capercaillie	Pintail	Snipe, Common
Coot	Plover, Golden	Teal
Duck, Tufted	Pochard	Wigeon
Mallard	Shoveler	Woodcock

THE PROTECTION OF WILD ANIMALS

The Wildlife and Countryside Act 1981 provides protection to wild animals and lists in Schedule 5 (see Appendix 4) those species which are specifically protected. These species are unlikely to be encountered whilst shooting, except for the red squirrel, bats and the otter.

Excluded methods for killing or taking any wild animal

It is illegal, however to use certain methods for killing or taking any wild animals. The sporting shotgun shooter should be aware that he is gulity of an offence if he:
(*i*) uses for the purpose of killing or taking any wild animal any self-locking snare, any bow or crossbow or any explosive other than ammunition for a firearm (including shotgun);
(*ii*) uses as a decoy, for the purpose of killing or taking any wild animal, any live mammal or bird.

However an open licence (this means you do not need to apply for it specifically) allows the keeping of birds in certain cage traps for pest control purposes. It's issue is reviewed annually.

Excluded methods for killing or taking Schedule 6 animals

Additionally, animals which appear in Schedule 6 may not be killed or taken by the following methods:
1. **Any semi-automatic weapon.**
2. **Any device for illuminating a target or sighting device for nightshooting.**
3. **Any form of artificial light or any mirror or other dazzling device.**

4. Use as a decoy, for the purpose of killing or taking any such wild animal, any sound recording.

5. Using any mechanically propelled vehicle in immediate pursuit of any such wild animal for the purpose of driving, killing or taking that animal.

The above methods 1–5 are by implication permitted for the purpose of taking or killing those animals which do not appear in Schedules 5 or 6.

SCHEDULE 6

Animals in Schedule 6 which are likely to be encountered whilst shooting:

Badger	Marten, Pine
Bats (all species)	Otter, Common
Cat, Wild	Polecat
Hedgehog	Squirrel, Red

NORTHERN IRELAND

THE SEASONS AND THE SCHEDULES

All birds, their eggs and nests are protected at all times by the Wildlife (Northern Ireland) Order 1985.

The Order, however, makes provision for certain species to be killed or taken at certain times by authorised persons.

*Schedule 2
Part I*

Birds in Schedule 2 Part I which may be killed or taken outside the close season:

Curlew	Pintail
Duck, Tufted	Plover, Golden
Gadwall	Pochard
Goldeneye	Scaup
Goose, Grey-lag	Shoveler
Goose, Pink-footed	Teal
Mallard	Wigeon

*Schedule 2
Part II*

Birds in Schedule 2 Part II which may be killed or taken by authorised persons at all times:

Crow, Hooded/Carrion	Magpie
Gull, Great black-backed	Pigeon, Feral
Gull, Herring	Pigeon, Wood
Gull, Lesser black-backed	Rook
Jackdaw	Sparrow, House
	Starling

Schedule 3

Birds which may be sold dead at all times:

Woodpigeon

i.e. the sale of any other dead wild bird is prohibited at all times.

N.B. It should be noted that only those species of birds listed in Schedule 2 Parts I and II may be killed or taken, all other species are protected, some by special penalties as listed in Schedule I.

Schedule 1
Part I

Lists those birds which are protected at all times by special penalties.

Schedule 1
Part II

Lists those birds which are protected by special penalties during the close season.

GAME BIRDS

The Wildlife (Northern Ireland) Order 1985 also defines 'game birds' as pheasant, partridge (including chukar partridge and red-legged partridge), woodcock, snipe and red grouse.

THE SHOOTING SEASONS IN NORTHERN IRELAND

THE OPEN AND CLOSE
SEASONS FOR GAME AND
WILDFOWL

(All dates inclusive)

Grouse	12 August–30 November
Cock pheasant*	1 October–31 January
Wild ducks, geese and waders†	1 September–31 January
Woodcock	1 October–31 January
Snipe	1 September–31 January
Hares	12 August–31 January

*Hen pheasants and grey partridge are protected at all times.
†Refers only to those birds which appear in Schedule 2 Part I of the Wildlife (N.I.) Order 1985.

THE GAME ACTS

ENGLAND, SCOTLAND
AND WALES

'Game' includes hares, pheasants, partridges, grouse, heath or moor game and black game.

THE GAME SEASONS

Pheasant	1 October – 1 February inclusive
Partridge	1 September – 1 February inclusive
Grouse/Ptarmigan	12 August – 10 December inclusive
Blackgame	20 August – 10 December inclusive
Hare	No season but may not be offered for sale from 1 March – 31 July inclusive

It is illegal to shoot any species out of season.
It is illegal to shoot game on Sundays, Christmas Day or at night.

LICENCES

Game Licences

It is illegal to shoot all game species, common snipe and woodcock without a Game Licence (but certain exceptions apply in the case of hares – see below).

Game Dealer's Licence

It is an offence to sell game without a licence.

Only a licensed dealer or a person having a licence to kill game may sell game; the latter only to a licensed game dealer. A gamekeeper with a Gamekeeper's Licence and his employer's written permission may sell game on behalf of his employer to a licensed game dealer.

An occupier of land may, under the provision of the Ground Game Act, sell hares killed on his land without either having a licence to kill or a licence to deal in, but only to a licensed dealer.

A Dealer's Licence is obtainable from the local Council; when this has been issued a futher licence must be obtained from a Money Order Post Office. Two licences are needed, one under the Game Act 1831 and the other an Excise Licence under the Game Licence Act 1860.

Hares

You do not require a Game Licence to shoot hares, provided that you are shooting on land where you are the owner (having the right to kill game), occupier or a person duly authorised in writing under the provisions of either the Hares Act 1848 or the Ground Game Acts.

Only one person can be so authorised and must be either:

1. A member of the occupier's household resident on the land;
2. A person in the occupier's ordinary service on the land;
3. A person genuinely employed for reward to kill and take hares and rabbits on the land.

NIGHT SHOOTING

Night is taken to mean the period from one hour after sunset to one hour before sunrise.

England and Wales

Rabbits may be shot at night by the landowner or by persons authorised by him.

Hares may be shot at night by authorised persons.

Game may not be shot at night.

Scotland

Rabbits and hares may be shot at night by authorised persons.

Game may not be shot at night.

Northern Ireland

It is illegal to shoot at night.

50

There is very little free shooting in this country, shooting rights will almost always be held by the landowner or shooting tenant and under a measure of control.

If you shoot anywhere without permission, you lay yourself open to prosecution for armed trespass or trespass in pursuit of game (poaching).

According to the circumstances, you can be charged with one or both of these offences.

Always ensure that you are authorised to shoot where you intend to go.

Wildfowling on the foreshore is often thought to be free shooting. It is not. The law, and the exceptions, are explained in detail in Chapter 9.

Whether peer or postman, tipster or tycoon,
Heed these words of warning otherwise you'll soon
Realise what happens in most every court –
'Ignorance of Law' can mean 'Farewell to your Sport'.
ANON

5   Behaviour in the Field

The following is a code of conduct regarding behaviour when in the field. More specific references to conduct when engaged in game shooting, wildfowling, and roughshooting occur in the respective sections.

Always remember that others will judge the sport by your behaviour and that of your companions.

If you observe others behaving in a manner likely to bring the sport into disrepute, politely but firmly bring their responsibility to the sport as a whole to their attention.

Always remember your responsibility to safeguard your quarry and its habitat for future generations.

Know the quarry species and their respective seasons.

Always ensure that you are authorised to shoot where you intend to go.

You must know precisely where the shoot boundaries are located.

Know the location of any public rights of way in the area.

Always advise the owner and/or the tenant in good time if you want to go shooting.

Check that it is convenient for you to go shooting at the time you intend to go. Check for restrictions which might affect your sport.

Always avoid causing unnecessary disturbance.

Avoid shooting at night where noise may be a nuisance.

Always respect the owner's property.

Respect crops, livestock, property and fences; damage to property may result in a loss of shooting rights.

Always open gates rather than climb them. Close gates after you, if they were closed initially. You may cut stock off from water by closing a gate intentionally left open. Climb a secured gate at the hinged end.

Do not break fences, rails or hedges.

Do not walk in standing corn; seek the farmer's guidance in respect of other growing crops.

Avoid disturbance to livestock.

Always keep your dog under control.

Do not let your dog disturb livestock. Sheep in lamb can be harmed if made to run; a dog need not chase sheep to cause them to panic. Schedule 7 of the Wildlife and Countryside Act 1981 and the Dogs (Protection of Livestock) Act 1953 make provision for the incurring of a penalty in law if a dog is allowed to worry livestock on agricultural ground or is at large (that is, not on a lead or otherwise under close control) in a field or enclosure in which there are sheep.

If quarry is shot and falls or runs over the boundary, it is proper to seek permission to retrieve it.

Always observe the BASC Shotgun Safety Code.

This is outlined in detail in Chapter 3. You should be thoroughly conversant with this.

Always remember that it is the sportsman's responsibility to understand the laws relating to his sport.

You must be aware of the laws relating to the sport, particularly to shotguns and to your quarry (see Chapter 4).

Always seek to present your quarry as a sporting shot.

Allow flushed quarry to gain reasonable distance – 14m (15yds).
Remember that it is equally unsporting to shoot at quarry which is out of range. Vermin shooting may be excepted in the case of close shots, **but out-of-range shooting at vermin is also inexcusable.**

Always ensure that your shooting is as good as possible.

You will improve your shooting by practice on clay pigeons. One recommended method of shooting a moving target is given in Appendix 5.

Always 'mark' by carefully watching wounded game and ensure that it is picked up without delay.

A trained gundog is recommended whenever you shoot.
Every conceivable effort should be made to locate, pick up and humanely despatch wounded quarry.

Always despatch wounded quarry as humanely and as quickly as possible.

A sharp knock on the head with a suitably heavy stick or 'priest' is most effective for birds.
Hares and rabbits can be killed by holding them by the head between the first and second fingers, with the first finger extended under the creature's chin, and quickly jerking the animal downwards, effecting a dislocation of the neck by the weight of the body.

Always observe the Code of Practice for safe gun-handling when despatching wounded quarry.

Always wear suitable and sensible clothing and footwear to suit your surroundings.

Make contingency plans for wet and cold weather and carry appropriate clothing.

Always ensure that your shotgun certificate is signed and valid.

Always ensure that you have a valid game licence if shooting at game.

Carry it and your shotgun certificate whenever you go out shooting.

Always take your quarry from the game bag as soon as possible.

Store it in a cool, fly-proof place. Do not waste it.

Always remember that the enjoyment of sport is not reflected by the size of the bag.

Do not over shoot. A viable breeding stock must be left on the ground at the end of the season. (Crop protection may be an exception.)

Never shoot a bird just because it is within range of your gun.

Although it may be in range of your gun, it may provide a more sporting shot for another gun.

Never leave litter.

Take all your litter home with you. This includes empty cartridge cases.

Whenever possible pick up litter left by someone else. Litter can be a hazard to livestock.

Never let excitement cloud your judgement.

Concentration and attention to safety are vital at all times.

The sportsman's responsibility is to ensure that he positively identifies his target before taking a shot.

It is essential that the sportsman should be able to distinguish rapidly between quarry and non-quarry species in the field. The primary aim of this guide is to help sportsmen to learn the techniques of species identification, with particular reference to the main quarry species. But the principles established apply equally to non-quarry species. Through practising field identification at every opportunity the sportsman will not only become competent at recognising his target species, he will also benefit from his ability to identify non-quarry animals.

Species identification is a craft, the skills for which are acquired through field experience.

It is important for the sportsman to have access to guides and texts to help him learn the characteristic field marks of both quarry and non-quarry species. It is equally important for him to appreciate that no amount of 'armchair identification' can substitute for field experience. This section is no more than an introductory guide. It is necessarily limited in scope, and covers only the most popular sporting quarry species. It should be supplemented by extensive practice of quarry identification under a wide range of field conditions, and used in conjunction with a more comprehensive field guide (a selection of the more popular field guides are listed on page 56). These field guides will help the sportsman to become more aware of non-quarry species—including those which occur in Britain only occasionally or in very small numbers. The experience gained through attempting to identify all species encountered, regardless of their quarry status and throughout the year, will enhance the sportsman's enjoyment of the countryside and eliminate the risks of shooting at non-quarry species.

HOW TO IDENTIFY QUARRY SPECIES

The aim of this guide is to establish the basic principles which enable the sportsman to recognise quarry species.

Quarry species comprise two groups of animals—birds and mammals. The features used to recognise the differences between these two groups of animals can be used to illustrate the basic principles of species identification. Birds are immediately recognisable by their feathers and wings, and mammals by their fur and four limbs. Species identification is simply an extension of the ability to recognise features which tell apart different species. Most people will almost instinctively be able to 'identify' an animal as being a bird or mammal—and many will be able to go one step further and define the type of, say, bird as a 'duck' or a 'pigeon'. Species identification is achieved through learning the key field-marks and behaviour which characterise particular groups and species from one another, and enable the animal under observation to be positively identified.

The features which provide the most useful clues to quarry identification are the animal's size, shape, markings, colour, general behaviour and distribution in both space and time.

Positive species identification usually results from a combination of the various diagnostic features.

The features which provide the most useful clues to quarry recognition are:

1. Size and shape
It is particularly important to use a familiar species as a guide for comparison with other species in the same group; and also to note any distinctive features of the animal's shape which permit identification in silhouette, including, in the case of birds, those features which are readily seen in flight.

2. Colour and pattern
Note any unique colouring, or patterns of colour, paying particular attention to markings which can be detected at long range.

3. Behaviour
Visual clues, such as the way an animal moves on the ground, a bird's flight or perching behaviour, and audible signals such as call-notes or the sounds created by wing-beats are all important in species recognition.

4. Habitat and seasonal pattern
As all species show some kind of preference where they feed or seek shelter, the kind of habitat gives some indication of the species which might be found in a particular area.

Knowledge of species' habitat preferences taken together with any seasonal migration movements enables the sportsman to anticipate, within broad limits, which species he is likely to encounter at a particular locality. But general distribution limits—such as 'normal' habitat and 'usual' range for example—cannot be used alone as diagnostic features.

Further reading

The list below contains a small selection from the wide range of field guides and other texts which will give the sportsman more information and guidance on the identification of British birds and mammals, and on the natural history of the main quarry species. Most of these books are inexpensive and widely available from bookshops.

FIELD IDENTIFICATION GUIDES

Birds

Hermann Heinzel, Richard Fitter and John Parslow: *The Birds of Britain and Europe*, Collins, London.

P.A.D. Hollom: *The Popular Handbook of British Birds*, Witherby, London.

Roger Peterson, Guy Mountfort and P. A. D. Hollom: *A Field Guide to the Birds of Britain and Europe*, Collins, London.

Mammals

G. B. Corbet and H. N. Southern: *The Handbook of British Mammals*, Blackwell, Oxford.

M. J. Lawrence and R. W. Brown: *Mammals of Britain: Their Tracks, Trails and Signs*, Blandford, Poole.

Specialised texts

Franklin Coombs: *The Crows*, Batsford, London.
M. A. Ogilvie: *Ducks of Britain and Europe*, Poyser, Berkhamsted.
Myrfyn Owen: *Wild Geese of the World*, Batsford, London.
A. J. Prater: *Estuary Birds of Britain and Ireland*, Poyser, Calton.

THE QUARRY SPECIES

The 35 most popular quarry animals which may, under current legislation, be pursued for sport by authorised persons are described in detail in this section.

Current legislation provides for open shooting seasons or shooting by authorised persons of 80 species of wild birds and terrestrial mammals in Britain. This includes both traditional sporting quarry species (wildfowl, gamebirds, hares, etc) and animals shot for pest control purposes (some gulls, rats and mustelids—stoats, weasels, etc), together with some species which fall into a grey area between the two categories (including crows, Woodpigeon and Rabbit).

Those animals regarded primarily as pest species are outside the scope of this volume, which is concerned only with the sporting quarry which may be taken with a shotgun. Thus, of the 38 birds which may be shot, the Great and Lesser Black-backed and Herring Gulls, Collared Dove, Feral Pigeon, Starling and House Sparrow are excluded. Of the mammals, only four species are considered to be targets for sporting shotgun shooting. Full details of the legal framework for shotgun shooting are given in Chapter 4 (The Law) and Appendix 4 to which the reader is referred for further information.

Quarry animals fall into several categories of similar species.

The 35 quarry animals (31 birds and 4 mammals) are grouped into the following categories of similar or closely related species.

WILDFOWL

These comprise ducks and geese, large numbers of which are migratory, visiting the British Isles during autumn and winter, returning in spring to northern breeding grounds.

Ducks

These are the most widespread and numerous wildfowl. Sexes are normally very dissimilar—the male (drake) is usually highly coloured, except in eclipse plumage, while the female (duck) has characteristically drab plumage throughout the year. The nine quarry species of ducks can be usefully divided in two groups according to their mode of feeding.

1. Dabbling ducks

This group comprises Mallard, Teal, Wigeon, Pintail, Shoveler and Gadwall. As their group name suggests, dabblers obtain food mainly from shallow water, paddling to stir up mud, etc. or 'up-ending' to sieve out food material from just below the surface. They tend to be agile on land. Mallard, Teal and Gadwall regularly feed on agricultural land, especially cereal stubbles in autumn; while Wigeon chiefly graze on grassland.

Species in this group are typified by the ease with which they take to the wing—an important escape strategy as birds frequently feed in small wetlands, damp woodlands, etc. Teal will rise almost vertically from the surface. All fly easily and show considerable agility on the wing.

Most dabblers are typically night-feeders. Their normal pattern is to use a safe roost site during the day, frequently on open water such as small- to medium-sized ponds, and flight to feeding areas at dusk, returning to their roost at dawn. This generalised pattern may be complicated by local weather and feeding conditions and will vary with different species. Those feeding on the foreshore, such as Wigeon grazing saltings, are governed largely by tidal cycles. Bright moonlight (which can occur under clear skies during full moon) resembles daylight and can result in a complex pattern of movements between roost site and intertidal feeding areas. This period of bright moonlit nights is also exploited by inland ducks which similarly flight between roost and feeding areas during the night.

2. Diving ducks

This group comprises Tufted Duck, Pochard and Goldeneye.

These species typically use deeper, open waters for both feeding and roosting, and one site can fulfil both functions. They dive to moderate depths to forage on plant or animal material from the water or bottom muds. Ducks in this group are highly adapted to swimming and as a result they move with less ease on land than dabbling ducks. They are also slower in taking to the wing, and have to patter along the surface to gain lift. Often they will swim away or dive to avoid danger, only taking flight as a last resort. They do flight to and from roost sites if these differ from feeding waters; and they often show a peak of activity in evening and early morning, resting in the middle of the night.

Geese

This group includes Britain's largest quarry bird species. They are divided into two groups. The 'grey' geese (*Anser* species) are Greylag, Pink-footed and White-fronted; they are basically grey and greyish-brown with typically fairly uniform plumage tones. The 'black' or 'dark' geese (*Branta* species) tend to have a contrasting black or dark brown with white or light grey colouring; the Canada Goose is the only quarry species in this group. Sexes are generally similar, and indistinguishable in the field. The young of all grey geese look rather similar, generally lacking

adult plumage characters, but as they tend to retain strong family ties during their first winter problems of identification are reduced. Geese typically feed during the day and roost at night; although, as with ducks, tidal cycles and moonlight will alter patterns of movement, especially of those species using tidal areas for feeding. Flocks (skeins) normally fly in V-formation or straggly lines. Their call notes are highly characteristic, and hence are very important in species recognition.

OTHER WATERBIRDS

Two species of the rail family—Moorhen and Coot—are found in a wide range of marsh and open water habitats. They are typified by bulky bodies and swim with a jerky action.

WADERS

Waders are a diverse group of birds. Golden Plover and Snipe occur in coastal marshes, inland wetlands and moors. The Woodcock is regarded as a 'forest wader' in view of its affinity to woodland habitats and close relationship to snipe. Sexes are generally indistinguishable in the field.

GAMEBIRDS

Gamebirds comprise two main groups, divided according to their habitat preferences. All gamebirds are characterised by their mode of flight. They are largely ground-dwelling birds, and tend to fly only when forced to do so. When flushed from cover they take off noisily. Once airborne their flight is strong, direct and often high, characterised by short bursts of whirring wing-beats alternating with gliding on down-curved wings.

Lowland gamebirds

These are Pheasant, Grey and Red-legged Partridges. Grey Partridge is native to Britain; the others are introduced species. All are closely associated with lowland agricultural and woodland

habitats. Pheasant and Red-legged Partridges are intensively managed to maintain high populations for sporting shooting purposes. This involves both habitat management (e.g. provision of cover) and species management (e.g. rearing and release of young, providing supplementary food etc). Grey Partridge populations are managed largely through the provision of suitable cover and forage.

Upland gamebirds

This group comprises four indigenous grouse species—Red and Black Grouse, Ptarmigan and Capercaillie. The last species was

previously extinct but was re-established from breeding stock introduced from Sweden during the nineteenth century. All four species have quite distinct and different habitat requirements. Red Grouse are characteristic of open heather moors; Capercaillie inhabit upland woodland—mainly pine forest; Black Grouse are found typically in moorland and forest-edge habitats and Ptarmigan on higher, rocky mountain tops.

PIGEONS AND DOVES

Three species are legal quarry, but only the Woodpigeon is considered to be a popular target for sport-shooting. It is frequently regarded as a pest by farmers in view of the large numbers which may congregate to feed on ripening or recently sown crops.

CORVIDS

The quarry species comprise Crow (which occurs as two distinct sub-species—Carrion and Hooded), Rook, Jackdaw, Magpie and Jay.

The crow family includes species which have long been regarded as a menace to game-rearing operations. Most are considered also to be popular sporting quarry. They have a varied diet, and readily adapt to exploit available food resources—hence the problems resulting from their predation on eggs and young birds in game-rearing sites. Sexes are similar, and indistinguishable in the field. Most populations are resident, but in some areas they undertake short movements outside the breeding season to avoid harsh weather, or involving the dispersal of young.

HARE AND RABBIT

These closely related herbivores are characterised by their long hind-legs and long ears. They are capable of high speed and rapid changes in direction while running.

The Brown and Mountain Hares are traditionally considered as game species. The Rabbit is frequently regarded as a pest species, but is also a sporting quarry.

SQUIRRELS

The Grey Squirrel is the only quarry species in this group. It is characterised by its long tail and arboreal habits. It is considered a sporting quarry, although it is most frequently shot to prevent damage to forestry and game interests.

USING THE QUARRY IDENTIFICATION GUIDE

Each species description concentrates on the features which enable the sportsman to make a positive identification of his quarry, together with information on its normal range and habitat preferences. A glossary of technical terms is given opposite.

BIRD TOPOGRAPHY

The parts of a bird referred to in the species accounts are labelled on the fictitious bird illustrated on this page. The annotated features are defined in the list below together with some aspects of plumage or anatomy which are not depicted on the diagram.

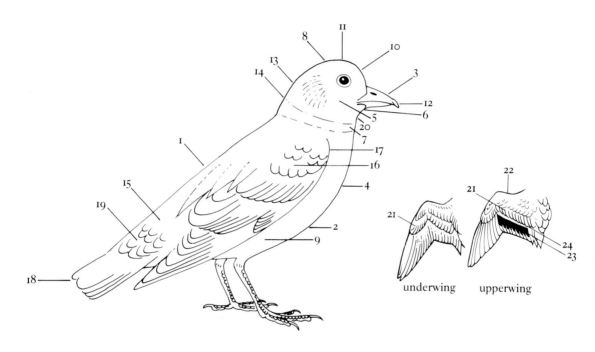

underwing   upperwing

Profile diagram

1 Back	10 Forehead	19 Tail coverts
2 Belly	11 Head	20 Throat
3 Bill	12 Nail	
4 Breast (Chest)	13 Nape	
5 Cheek	14 Neck	*Wing Detail*
6 Chin	15 Rump	21 Coverts
7 Collar	16 Scapulars	22 Forewing
8 Crown	17 Shoulder	23 Speculum
9 Flank	18 Tail	24 Wing-bar

Features not illustrated
Frontal shield: hard, bare plate extending from top of bill over forehead.
Wattle: an area of bare, usually bright coloured flesh below throat.

The more technical terms used, mainly in connection with behaviour or habitat, are defined.

Arboreal tree-dwelling species.

Brackish intermediate between fresh and salt (sea) water.

Crepuscular active during twilight hours.

Diurnal active during daylight hours.

Eclipse the dull plumage of adult male ducks in late summer, at which time they are rendered temporarily flightless as they moult their flight feathers.

Feral wild population originating from introduced stocks (released or escaped animals).

Form shallow depression or 'nest'-scrape of hares.

Gregarious found in association with others of the same species.

Herbivore species which feeds by grazing vegetation.

Lek traditional site for male courtship displays during spring.

Maritime coastal environment.

Migrant a species whose regular movement between summer (breeding) range and wintering grounds involves a substantial part of the population crossing national frontiers; 'passage migrant' describes a species which passes through a country en route between the countries in which its breeding and wintering grounds are located.

Moult loss and renewal of bird's feathers—normally occurs at least once each year. (See also *Eclipse*.)

Moult-migration movement of birds to areas where they can moult safely—applies in particular to ducks and geese with temporary flightless period.

Nocturnal active during hours of darkness.

Passage migrant (see under *Migrant*).

Predator species which kills individuals of other species for food.

Resident species remaining within the same country (but not necessarily the same locality) throughout the year.

Roding courtship behaviour of male Woodcock patrolling breeding habitat during spring and summer.

Roost main period of rest in a bird's 24-hour cycle of activity (not necessarily involving true sleep, and frequently during daylight as well as at night); also describes the place where birds settle to rest.

Saline salt water.

Sedentary species in which individuals normally remain in the same locality throughout the year.

Solitary normally found alone (or in breeding season as isolated pairs).

Terrestrial land-dwelling.

QUARRY SPECIES

In the following species descriptions, the vernacular (common) name of each species is followed by its scientific (Latin) name. Size refers to the average length of the adult animal from tip of its bill/nose to tail, with ranges given for species with marked size variation or significant differences between the sexes. Each species is shown in full colour.

To aid flight identification, monochrome figures of ducks in flight are included with each species description, and normal flock patterns are shown on pages 100–1.

Key to symbols

♂♀ Symbols for male (♂) and female (♀) are used throughout this section.

Key to maps

The maps depict the distribution of quarry species in Britain. These generalised maps show, as far as possible, the normal range of resident species, plus the breeding and main winter distributions of migrant species. Migratory movements and dispersal of some species are quite complex; to avoid over complicating the maps some distributions, such as the influx of Woodpigeons from the Continent or Hooded Crows into eastern England, are omitted. The primary aim is to present a simple guide for the sportsman, to indicate the main distribution of quarry species during the shooting season.

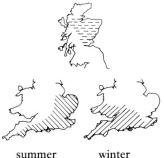

Sedentary and mainly resident species are denoted by dashed lines.

Migratory species, and residents whose populations are supplemented in winter by a significant number of immigrants, are denoted by cross-hatched lines.

summer   winter

Key to shooting season block

The open season is shaded, and dates of opening and closing are specified. All information refers to Britain (England, Scotland and Wales) unless otherwise specified. (Details of shooting seasons, local restrictions, authorisation, etc are given in Chapters 4, 8 and 9.)

Examples:

1. Typical open season for duck: opens 1 September; closes on 31 January inland and 20 February on foreshore.

J	F	M	A	M	J	J	A	S	O	N	D
	31				INLAND						
	20				FORESHORE			1			

2. Woodcock: season opens 1 September (in Scotland), 1 October (England and Wales); closes 31 January (all Britain).

J	F	M	A	M	J	J	A	S	O	N	D
	31			ENGLAND & WALES				1			
				SCOTLAND			1				

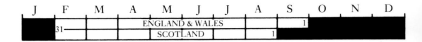

MALLARD

Anas platyrhynchos
size: 58 cm (23 in)

Large dabbling duck. Adult ♂ characterised by glossy, dark green head, white collar and purple-brown chest; rest of plumage mainly light grey, tail white with black central feathers. ♀ dull, mottled brown. Both sexes have purple speculum bordered by white wing-bars, particularly conspicuous in flight. Juvenile similar to ♀.

Voice: ♀ has characteristic loud, deep *quark* either uttered singly (often in alarm) or several strung together during courtship. ♂ quieter; typical call a soft, nasal *quark* and high whistle.

One of the most widespread of British breeding birds, and the most numerous breeding waterfowl. Frequents a very wide variety of predominantly still, shallow freshwater and brackish wetlands, from small ponds and large reservoirs to marshes, rivers, park lakes and canals. Outside breeding season extends into maritime habitats. Captive-bred birds released on a large scale to supplement wild stock. Breeding population mainly resident; local movements and dispersal of young predominate, although released stock recorded as migrants as far afield as U.S.S.R. Passage migrants and winter visitors include immigrants from Iceland, Scandinavia, northern U.S.S.R. and north-central Europe, but chiefly from Baltic and North Sea countries; normally present September/October to April/May, widespread throughout the country in both coastal and inland areas.

Habitat and distribution

Typically feeds at night, resting by day at safe roost sites. Rises easily and almost vertically from water when flushed; flies quickly with shallow wing-beats. Flies in loose flocks, pairs or singly. Highly gregarious; ♂♂ flock during breeding season, while ♀ incubates; large flocks occur in autumn and winter.

Diet very varied, including wide range of plant and animal material; highly opportunistic feeder. Food obtained from water by sieving and pecking at surface, up-ending, and diving. Usually nests in undergrowth close to water; readily accepts artificial nest structures.

Behaviour and feeding

Colouring of ♂ resembles ♂ Red-breasted Merganser (protected). ♀ similar to ♀♀ of other dabbling duck species, particularly Gadwall, Pintail, Shoveler and Wigeon, but both ♂ and ♀ are bigger and more heavily-built than other dabbling ducks.

Similar species

J	F	M	A	M	J	J	A	S	O	N	D
	31			INLAND							
	20			FORESHORE		1					

Shooting season

65

TEAL

Anas crecca
size: 36 cm (14 in)

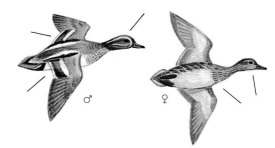

Field identification

Very small, compact dabbling duck. ♂ characterised by conspicuous grey plumage contrasting with dark chestnut head, creamy-buff patch on each side of black under-tail coverts and prominent white stripe along scapulars; at close quarters broad green patch extending from in front of eye to nape bordered by narrow buff line is evident; breast cream spotted with black; underside white. Speculum of both sexes green and black, bordered white. ♀ plumage mottled brown with paler cheeks and whitish underside. Juvenile similar to ♀, but more spotted under-parts. *Voice*: ♂ has characteristic low, whistling *crick-crick*; ♀ generally silent, but utters harsh *quack* in alarm.

Habitat and distribution

Breeding birds favour rushy moorland and heathland pools, bogs, etc, typically around small upland waters, but frequently well away from open water; in lowland areas prefers small lakes, rivers, fresh and brackish marshes with good cover. Requires shallow muddy water areas for feeding. In winter and on passage extends to coastal habitats (estuarine flats, salt-marshes, etc) also larger freshwater areas.
British breeding population largely resident, moving south or south-west in autumn. Some emigration from southern England to western Europe and Mediterranean. Large influx of passage migrants and winter immigrants originate from Iceland, Baltic and North Sea countries, Scandinavia and northern U.S.S.R.; main winter concentrations are in south-east England; immigrants appear from the end of August to November, returning March to early May.

Behaviour and feeding

Extremely agile in flight, frequently in tight packs; rises vertically from water or land and flies fast with characteristic very rapid wing-beats; long distance flights normally high, in lines or V-formation. Gregarious outside breeding season, often in small flocks; more dispersed in small parties, pairs or singly while feeding. Feeds primarily at night, often moving several miles from safe day-time roost to feeding area. Food obtained by dabbling in shallow, muddy water. Diet varies according to season and locality; seeds predominate in autumn and winter; increasing amount of animal material taken in summer.
Nests in thick cover on ground, normally close to water.

Similar species

Only species of similar size is Garganey (protected) – a summer visitor.

Shooting season

J	F	M	A	M	J	J	A	S	O	N	D
	31				INLAND						
	20				FORESHORE		1				

WIGEON
Anas penelope
size: 46 cm (18 in)

Medium-sized, short-necked dabbling duck. Basic plumage colour of ♂ is grey, with buff forehead and crown and remainder of head chestnut; chest pinkish-brown, white under-parts; characteristic white shoulder patch readily seen in flight. ♀ duller; brown plumage tinged rufous, white underside, green speculum fringed with white wing-bars. Short bill and dark pointed tail useful diagnostic characters.
Voice: highly distinctive whistling *whee-oo* of ♂, typically heard from flocks in flight; ♀♀ virtually silent.

Field identification

Small British breeding population restricted to upland lochs, pools and streams in open moorland, bogs and wooded country. Chiefly maritime outside breeding season, mainly on mud-flats and saltings; recently taken to inland flood-meadows especially in eastern England.
British population mostly resident, moving to coast in autumn with some south-westerly movements to Ireland. Passage migrants and winter immigrants, chiefly from Iceland, Scandinavia and northern U.S.S.R., mainly present September to April. Occurs in large numbers, particularly in east and south-east England, south-west and north-east Scotland.

Habitat and distribution

Highly gregarious outside breeding season. Very large feeding flocks occur; often roosts in large numbers on sea, sand-flats, etc. Usually roosts during day, feeding at night, but may reverse pattern depending on prevailing tidal and weather conditions. Grazes predominantly on grasses, usually while walking over exposed vegetation, but frequently feeds from water surface. Takes mainly leaves, stems, roots, etc of grasses and herbs, seeds and some animal material.
Nests on ground in heather, bracken or rank grasses.

Behaviour and feeding

♀ resembles other ♀ dabbling ducks, especially Shoveler, Pintail, Gadwall and Mallard.

Similar species

J	F	M	A	M	J	J	A	S	O	N	D
	31			INLAND							
	20			FORESHORE			1				

Shooting season

67

PINTAIL

Anas acuta
size: 56 cm (22 in)

♀   ♂

Field identification

Large, slim-built dabbling duck with noticeably long neck and extended central pair of tail feathers forming characteristic needle-tail of ♂, and shorter but still pointed tail of ♀. ♂ has dark brown head, and back of neck, contrasting with pure white breast, sides and front of neck, extending as white streak up side of head; under-parts white; back and flanks light grey; rump black; wings grey and brown with green speculum conspicuous in flight. ♀ duller, with grey-brown plumage and no discernible wing-pattern in flight, except a light trailing edge to inner wing. Juvenile resembles ♀, but generally darker and more uniform.
Voice: generally silent; ♂ has low Teal-like whistle, ♀ has a hoarse *quack*.

Small British breeding population widely distributed in a diverse range of habitats, including moorland pools, freshwater marshes and damp, rough grassland in low-lying areas.
In winter chiefly a coastal species, found mainly in estuarine and other sheltered coastal areas; also on inland flood-lands and freshwater marshes, and sometimes agricultural land.
Mainly migratory; British breeding birds move south, but possibly remain within Britain; augmented in autumn by passage migrants and winter visitors from Iceland, Scandinavia and north-western U.S.S.R.
Immigrants appear in mid-September, departing in April.

Habitat and distribution

Behaviour and feeding

Highly gregarious outside breeding season; flocks vary in size from small parties to several thousands on larger waters. Typically feeds at night and remains relatively inactive during daylight. Swims high on water; feeds mainly by up-ending or dabbling. Flight is fast and direct with rapid wing-beats; often fly in long lines or V-formation.
Diet includes a wide variety of plant and animal material, chiefly from bottom mud in shallow water. Will also feed on stubble grain or dig plant roots and underground stems.
Nests on ground usually in short cover; often in loose colonies; primarily on islands in lakes and adjacent to moorland pools.

Similar species

Although ♂ readily distinguished, ♀ resembles other ♀ dabbling ducks, particularly Mallard, Gadwall, Shoveler and Wigeon.

J	F	M	A	M	J	J	A	S	O	N	D
	31			INLAND							
	20			FORESHORE			1				

Shooting season

68

SHOVELER

Anas clypeata
size: 51 cm (20 in)

Medium-sized dabbling duck; both sexes characterised by enormous spatulate bill, large head and short neck, which are readily discernible both in flight and on the water. ♂ has striking pattern of dark green head, chestnut flanks and belly contrasting with pure white chest, which is noticeable at considerable distances; pale blue forewing, green speculum edged with white. ♀ primarily mottled brown, with similar but duller blue forewing and green speculum. Juvenile a dull version of ♀.
Voice: generally silent outside breeding season.

Field identification

Breeding population thinly but widely distributed; main concentration in southern and eastern England. Restricted chiefly to shallow, nutrient-rich fresh and brackish waters throughout the year. British birds migrate south to France, Spain and into Africa; large numbers pass through Britain on migration; smaller numbers overwinter. Immigrants and passage migrants originate from Iceland, Scandinavia and U.S.S.R. Local birds normally leave by late October; main passage through Britain occurs in November; main return movements March/April.

Habitat and distribution

Characteristic appearance when swimming, with front end carried low and huge bill angled down. Feeds primarily by swimming with head and neck submerged and surface feeding, moving head from side-to-side filtering out food particles; occasionally up-ends. Diet varied, including microscopic animals, seeds and other plant material. Predominately a day-time feeder usually singly, in pairs or small flocks. Flight agile with rapid wing-beats; makes loud whistling noise in flight; wings appear set well-back on body; rises easily from water with characteristic drumming sound. Particularly active on the wing in April.
Nests usually close to water, on ground in variety of habitats from rushes to open, short grassland and low scrub.

Behaviour and feeding

Huge bill distinctive, but plumage of ♀ similar to that of ♀ Gadwall, Pintail, Mallard and Wigeon.

Similar species

Shooting season

69

GADWALL

Anas strepera
size: 51 cm (20 in)

Field identification

Medium-sized dabbling duck. ♂ has uniform grey-brown plumage and conspicuous black rump; distinctive white speculum forms a bold white patch on trailing edge of wing, readily seen in flight; wing coverts chestnut and black. ♀ dull, mottled brown, with white belly and white wing-patch as ♂. Juvenile much like ♀, but well marked with streaks and spots on underside and darker upper-parts.
Voice: ♀ has high-pitched *quack*; ♂ has a short nasal call.

Prefers shallow, nutrient-rich, sheltered lakes, slow-moving streams, and freshwater marshes of lowland Britain; outside breeding season also found on brackish and saline waters. Establishment in Britain as a breeding species aided by escapes from collections and release of captive-bred birds. English population mainly resident, but Scottish birds move southwards to England and Ireland and some movement of birds from East Anglia to western Europe and Mediterranean. Winter visitors chiefly from Iceland, Baltic and North Sea countries; arrive mainly October/November, returning March/April.

Habitat and distribution

Behaviour and feeding

Tends to be fairly secretive and retiring throughout year; rarely gathers in large flocks; frequently mixes in small numbers with other dabbling ducks. Swims high in water; very mobile on both land and water, as well as in air. Flies with rapid beats of apparently pointed wings, producing whistling sound in flight. Normally a day-time feeder; may spend much time flying between roost and feeding sites. Feeds mainly on aquatic plant material, obtained either by swimming with head under water or dabbling; also steals food from other waterbirds; will occasionally feed on land, grazing and taking grain from stubble fields.
Nests on ground, close to water in very dense vegetation.

Similar species

Size close to that of Mallard; ♀ plumage resembles ♀ Mallard, Pintail, Wigeon and Shoveler.

J	F	M	A	M	J	J	A	S	O	N	D
	31				INLAND						
	20				FORESHORE		1				

Shooting season

70

TUFTED DUCK

Aythya fuligula
size: 43 cm (17 in)

Field identification

Small diving duck. Adult ♂ black with white flanks and belly; long, thin, drooping crest. ♀ rich dark brown head and back; flanks and underside paler; crest shorter than in adult ♂. In flight both sexes appear black with white belly and a distinctive broad white wing-bar. Juvenile resembles ♀.
Voice: virtually silent except during courtship.

Frequents open fresh waters of all sizes. During breeding season prefers more secluded, small- to moderate-sized lakes, particularly with fringing reeds or similar cover and vegetated islands. In winter readily takes to larger open waters such as reservoirs. Rarely found on sea. Widespread breeding species throughout lowland areas of British Isles. Marked range extension and population increase in recent decades; readily colonises new breeding habitats created by gravel excavation, etc. In winter local populations show some southerly movement within the country. British population augmented by birds from Iceland, northern and western Europe. Immigrants usually arrive mid-September/mid-November, depart late February/mid-May, and are found throughout the country, with notable concentrations on reservoirs in south and east England.

Habitat and distribution

Frequently uses same water area for both feeding and roosting, thus avoiding need to flight to and from feeding sites. Feeds mainly morning and evening. Normally shifts position if disturbed before flighting off water. Patters for some distance on take-off; flight usually straight and rapid, with quick beats of short wings. Dives in generally shallow waters; food mainly animal material, supplemented by vegetation (grasses, duckweed, etc).
Nests typically close to water in bushes or rushes; occasionally found in loose colonies, especially on islands.

Behaviour and feeding

♂ resembles ♂ Scaup (protected); ♀ similar to ♀ Pochard and Scaup (protected).

Similar species

J	F	M	A	M	J	J	A	S	O	N	D
	31			INLAND							
	20			FORESHORE		1					

Shooting season

71

POCHARD

Aythya ferina
size: 46 cm (18 in)

♂   ♀

Field identification

Habitat and distribution

Behaviour and feeding

Medium-sized diving duck with 'dumpy' appearance on water. ♂ has dark chestnut head and neck contrasting with pale grey back and flanks, black breast and tail. ♀ uniform dull brown, slightly paler around face. Both sexes characterised in flight by absence of white on wings; pale grey wing-bar runs full length of wing, forewing dark grey. Juvenile resembles ♀.
Voice: virtually silent except during courtship.

Sparse British breeding population favours larger lowland lakes, sluggish streams, etc, with dense fringing vegetation, and preferably islands. Found on larger freshwater areas, such as reservoirs, in winter; rarely in brackish or maritime habitats. Most British birds resident, but move away from breeding areas in winter; some emigrate to west Europe and Mediterranean. Passage migrants and winter visitors occur mainly during October to April; widely distributed, but with large concentrations in central lowlands of Scotland, central and southern England.

Gregarious outside breeding season, normally in small parties, occasionally flocks of several thousands. Spends most of time on water; take-off from water laboured, but when airborne has strong, fast flight with rapid beats of short wings making whistling sound. Flocks normally fly in tight group; long distance flights in lines or V-formation. Rarely occurs on land. Roosts during day in flocks on open water; feeds chiefly after dark in evening and early morning, less actively in middle of night. Diet mainly vegetable matter, including seeds, stems, leaves, etc, obtained normally by diving, occasionally by up-ending in shallower water; some animal material taken.
Nests on ground, normally in thick cover close to water; frequently by or on water, elevated above surface on rush or reed base.

Similar species

♂ readily distinguished; ♀ resembles ♀ Tufted Duck and Scaup (protected).

Shooting season

J	F	M	A	M	J	J	A	S	O	N	D
	31				INLAND						
	20				FORESHORE			1			

72

$♀$ $♂$

GOLDENEYE
Bucephala clangula
size: 46 cm (18 in)

Medium-sized diving duck. ♂ has high-crowned, dark head with greenish-purple gloss and circular white patch on cheek; neck and under-parts white contrasting with black back and rump and grey tail; extensive white on inner wing readily seen in flight. ♀ smaller than ♂; has chocolate-brown head, pale blue-grey upper-parts with white under-parts, grey flanks and tail; wings dark with conspicuous white patch similar to ♂. Juvenile closely resembles ♀.
Voice: generally silent, except during courtship display.

Field identification

Breeding habitat is tall forests close to moderately deep, productive open waters. During passage and on migration will make use of a variety of open water – lakes, reservoirs, streams, estuaries, etc. Migratory, but small British breeding population possibly undertakes only local movements; immigrants, mainly from Scandinavia, arrive from mid-September and return March/early May.

Habitat and distribution

Behaviour and feeding

Gregarious outside breeding season, normally in small flocks; spends most time on water or in flight, rarely comes to land. Mainly diurnal feeder; roost frequently considerable distance from feeding area. Flies with rapid wing-beats creating a characteristic loud whistling. Feeds chiefly on animal material, especially molluscs, crustaceans and insect larvae, obtained by diving to middle depths or bottom of feeding water. Nests in holes in trees; readily takes to nest boxes.

Both sexes readily distinguished from other diving-duck species.

Similar species

J	F	M	A	M	J	J	A	S	O	N	D
	31			INLAND							
	20			FORESHORE			1				

Shooting season

73

GREYLAG GOOSE

Anser anser
size: 75–90 cm (30–35 in)

Field identification

The largest grey goose. Head, neck and most of body uniform pale brownish-grey. Characterised by large size, heavy head and neck with stout bill, and very pale blueish-grey forewing – the latter especially obvious in flight. Bill bright orange with no black, and a white nail, legs flesh-pink. Breast often spotted with black. Young birds similar to adults, but generally unspotted, with greyer legs.
Voice: like domestic goose; a deep, loud nasal call; flight call loud, characteristically a deep cackle.

Habitat and distribution

In summer grazes in a variety of wetland habitats from lakes and marshes, agricultural pasture, to upland bogs and moorland. British breeding birds mostly resident. In autumn and winter immigrants generally found on agricultural pasture and cultivated land, marshes and estuaries. Some local movements of breeding populations occur; main influx of Icelandic breeding birds occurs in late October, and departure is generally mid-April. Highest concentration of immigrants is found in east-central Scotland.

Behaviour and feeding

Flight rapid and powerful, with regular beats of broad wings; characteristic circular flutter of wings on landing; takes off with ease from ground, although with more difficulty from water.
Usually flights from roosts to feeding grounds in early morning. Gregarious outside breeding season. Largest flocks usually occur in autumn when feeding on stubble and potato fields. Often found in mixed flocks with Pink-footed Geese where winter ranges overlap. Feeds almost entirely on plant material, normally grazing on land, but will feed on water, up-ending for submerged material. In autumn and winter normally feeds on grassland, cereal root crops, etc; late spring diet includes growing cereals.
Nests on ground either amongst heather (Scottish moors and bogs) or in bushes, reedbeds or other dense vegetation providing shelter; especially on islands; often colonial and rarely far from water.

Similar species

Can be confused with Bean (protected), Pink-footed and White-fronted Geese (especially immature birds), but all are smaller and more slightly built by comparison; calls are also distinctive.

J	F	M	A	M	J	J	A	S	O	N	D
	31				INLAND						
	20				FORESHORE				1		

Shooting season

74

PINK-FOOTED GOOSE

Anser brachyrhynchus
size: 60–76 cm (24–30 in)

Medium-sized, grey goose characterised by dark head and neck, contrasting with pale brownish body. Bill is small and short, dark coloured with a pink band; feet and legs are pink. Back and wings grey; paler forewing noticeable in flight. Young birds darker and more uniform above, mottled appearance below compared with more uniform colouring of adults.

Voice: characteristic short, high-pitched flight notes; also lower, more musical nasal calls.

Field identification

Breeding range in Arctic, from east Greenland and Iceland to Spitzbergen. Birds visiting Britain originate from Iceland and Greenland, nesting in coastal area of north-east Greenland and south-central Iceland. Winters in northern Britain and Ireland, with main concentrations in eastern Scotland. Arrives in September/October and departs April or early May. Found mainly on arable land, roosting on sand- and mud-flats in estuaries, inland lochs or reservoirs in moorland adjoining feeding areas.

Habitat and distribution

Autumn and winter flocks may comprise several thousand birds. Tend to feed by day but occasionally (especially under full moon) will stay out well into night or flight out to feed by night and roost during the day. Roost sites may be several miles from feeding area. During autumn feed mainly on barley stubble and potatoes. Pastures used throughout winter, and in spring feeds exclusively on grass and winter cereals; carrots and brassicas are taken in some districts.

Behaviour and feeding

Can be confused with Greylag, Bean (protected) and White-fronted Geese (especially immature birds); voices are characteristic.

Similar species

J	F	M	A	M	J	J	A	S	O	N	D
	31			INLAND							
	20			FORESHORE		1					

Shooting season

75

WHITE-FRONTED GOOSE

Anser albifrons
size: 66–76 cm (26–30 in)

Two races of the White-fronted Goose regularly occur in the British Isles, the European White-front (*Anser a. albifrons*) and Greenland White-front (*A. a. flavirostris*). The two sub-species are distinguishable in the field and have markedly different winter ranges (see distribution map). The following description relates to the European White-front, as current legislation does not provide for an open season for White-fronts in Scotland where the majority of the Greenland sub-species occur.

Field identification

Greenland population

European population

Medium-sized grey goose characterised by white band at base of upper bill and black barring on belly. Amount of black on underside extremely variable. Young birds lack these characters, but are normally found in the company of adults. Generally dark greyish-brown plumage, fairly long, pink bill, orange legs.
Voice: generally noisy species; typically high-pitched, musical cackle; flight call normally two or three syllable, short metallic notes.

Habitat and distribution

Breeding range in northern Siberia, within the Arctic Circle. Western section of population winters in Baltic and North Sea countries. Winter haunts in Britain located in south and east-central Wales and in southern England (Greenland White-front occurs in Scotland, Ireland and a few localities in west-central Wales). Arrives during October to January; departs March/April. Found mainly in lowland wet grasslands and marshes, arable fields, etc.

Behaviour and feeding

Normally feeds during day, usually close to roost and in undisturbed conditions will roost on feeding area. Congregate on arable land in autumn, feeding primarily on grass and stubble grain. Other food recorded includes potatoes, weed seeds, and clover. Flight noticeably more easy than other grey geese; quicker and more agile on the wing, and can take off almost vertically when disturbed. Large flocks gather on migration, but tends to split more readily into family parties and smaller groups than other grey geese.

Similar species

Can be confused with Greylag, Bean (protected) and Pink-footed Geese (especially immature birds), but generally distinguished by small size, uniformly dark plumage, and distinctive 'musical' call notes.

Shooting season
ENGLAND & WALES ONLY:
PROTECTED IN SCOTLAND

J	F	M	A	M	J	J	A	S	O	N	D
	31				INLAND					1	
	20				FORESHORE						

76

CANADA GOOSE

Branta canadensis
size: 91–102 cm (36–40 in)

Very large grey-brown goose; black head and neck with distinctive white patch extending from the chin across cheeks to behind the eye. Body dark above; paler brown flanks and under-parts; tail-coverts white, tail black. Bill and legs black. Young birds similar to adult, and generally indistinguishable in field.

Voice: considerable variety of calls, but flight note is characteristically a deep, loud, resonant, trumpeting honk.

Field identification

Introduced to England from North America in 17th century. Feral population generally resident, but local movements occur outside breeding season, and moult-migration to Scotland has evolved in Yorkshire sub-population since 1950s. Found in variety of lowland wetland habitats from ornamental park lakes (where first established) to freshwater marshes, gravel pits, etc; frequently close to human habitation.

Habitat and distribution

Feeds mostly during day; grass is prime constituent of diet throughout the year, supplemented by some insect matter in summer. Will also take clover and cereals; and sometimes up-end in water to feed on submerged vegetation. Gregarious, especially outside breeding season. Flight fast, with deep, regular wing-beats; often flies at low levels. Frequently walks from roost site to feeding area.

Usually nests on ground; prefers islands in open waters or marshes. Nest is normally under bushes or other sheltered spot. Frequently colonial, but pairs highly territorial and aggressive.

Behaviour and feeding

Not easily confused with other species of geese. The largest European goose: much larger than Brent and Barnacle (both protected), with characteristic black and white pattern on head and neck.

Similar species

J	F	M	A	M	J	J	A	S	O	N	D
	31				INLAND						
	20				FORESHORE			1			

Shooting season

77

MOORHEN

Gallinula chloropus
size: 33 cm (13 in)

Field identification

Habitat and distribution

Behaviour and feeding

Similar species

Small-sized, dark waterbird. Striking white flank stripes and under-tail coverts contrast with dark brownish to black upper-parts and slate-grey under-parts. Bill and frontal shield bright red; yellow bill tip. Sexes similar; juveniles brownish with creamy flank stripes, white under-tail coverts and greenish-brown bill.
Voice: loud call notes include a sharp metallic *krick*.

Breeding habitats include a wide variety of freshwater environments throughout most of the country; particularly in smaller ponds, ditches, sluggish streams, etc, but also in reed-beds, damp meadows, and larger lakes often in towns and cities. Frequently feeds away from water in adjacent grassland, etc. Found on larger waters outside breeding season. Most British birds resident, but local movements occur; some immigrants from western Europe occur mainly in eastern England during autumn and winter.

Solitary, in pairs or small parties; may gather into larger flocks during winter. Swims with jerky head action and tail cocked; flicks tail when anxious. Quite reluctant to fly, often seeking cover when disturbed; takes off from water by pattering along surface; flies low and fast with rapid wing-beats and trailing legs. May roost in trees and bushes. Feeds in water, pulling plant material, etc from surface, or walking through damp grassland. Diet varied; includes leaves, grass, seeds and fruit, also insects, eggs, earthworms, slugs, small fish, etc.
Nest usually in aquatic vegetation cover at waterside or close to water in adjacent undergrowth; normally constructed of dead reeds, sedge, etc.

Only likely to be confused with Coot.

J	F	M	A	M	J	J	A	S	O	N	D
	31						1				

Shooting season

COOT

Fulica atra
size: 38 cm (15 in)

Medium-sized bulky waterbird, characterised by overall very dark slate-grey body colour and black head in sharp contrast to white bill and frontal shield. On water distinguished by rounded back and apparently small head. Sexes similar; juvenile dark brown above, pale brown and whitish under-parts.
Voice: call a loud, sharp *kowk*.

Field identification

Inhabits mainly lowland open waters and slow-flowing streams. Normally requires minimum of a half hectare (one acre) of open water for breeding territory. Prefers shallow, nutrient-rich waters. Very large flocks occur in winter on reservoirs and other large expanses of open water, especially in southern England. British breeding population largely resident, with some movement away from higher altitudes and northern areas outside breeding season. European birds overwinter in large numbers, mainly in eastern and southern England.

Habitat and distribution

Highly territorial and aggressive in breeding season; gregarious at other times, winter flocks often congregating into large rafts. Swims and dives easily; normally reluctant to fly, but when forced to do so takes off from water by pattering along the surface in the manner of diving ducks. Flight normally low and ungainly with neck and legs extended; generally only flies for short distances. Obtains food mainly by diving to collect plant material from middle or lower depths; dives prolonged and food brought to surface to be consumed. In winter will also graze on damp grassland areas close to open water. Diet mainly leaves, stems, etc. of aquatic plants, also some animal material.
Nest normally among aquatic vegetation fringing open water; constructed of dead leaves from tall marsh plants.

Behaviour and feeding

Only likely to be confused with Moorhen; frequently associates with diving ducks, but readily distinguished from these.

Similar species

J	F	M	A	M	J	J	A	S	O	N	D
	31					1					

Shooting season

GOLDEN PLOVER

Pluvialis apricaria
size: 28 cm (11 in)

WINTER PLUMAGE

Field identification

Medium-sized wader with short, straight bill and rounded head. Distinguished at all seasons by rich gold and black spotted plumage on back and wings, white under-wing, and dark tail; no wing-bar. Face and under-parts in summer black with yellowish-white fringing stripe from forehead and neck to flanks. In winter underside and face whitish, mottled gold-brown. Juveniles more uniform than adults, paler above and darker below.
Voice: call note and characteristic clear, liquid *tlui* uttered in alarm, and normally in flight.

Habitat and distribution

Breeding birds typically haunt flat or gently undulating moorlands, upland grass-heaths and peat bogs. Move from hills in winter to lowland farmland and coastal habitats, occurring on arable and pasture farmland, estuaries, etc. British population largely resident, moving to lowlands and coasts; supplemented by passage migrants and winter visitors mainly from Iceland and Scandinavia, during September to April or May.

Behaviour and feeding

Gregarious outside breeding season; normally found in flocks, frequently in association with Lapwings (protected) on inland roosts and feeding sites. Flock flies in compact group; flight rapid and very agile. On ground has upright stance when still; walks with rapid steps tilting to gather food items. Diet varied; mainly insects, worms, crustaceans, seeds, berries, etc.
Nests on ground in short heather or grass heath.

Similar species

Confusion most likely with Grey Plover (protected), which is a winter visitor to coastal areas of Britain.

Shooting season

J	F	M	A	M	J	J	A	S	O	N	D
	31						1				

SNIPE

Gallinago gallinago
size: 27 cm (10½ in)

Small, brown wader with characteristic long, straight bill. Upper-parts rufous brown and black with golden-buff stripes on head and back; under-parts buff with dark brown markings and pale barred flanks. Juvenile resembles adult.
Voice: when flushed normally utters sharp, grating call note.

Field identification

Breeding habitat is typically wet grassland, bogs, marshes, etc, occasionally drier moorland sites. In winter frequents a wide variety of wetlands, including freshwater and salt-marshes, usually in lowland areas. Breeding birds largely resident, undergoing local movements mainly to lower ground, with some emigration to western Europe. Passage migrants and winter visitors occur, frequently in large numbers, during September to April, originating chiefly from Iceland, Scandinavia, Baltic states and western U.S.S.R.

Habitat and distribution

Generally secretive. Normally rests during day in rank vegetation, feeding most actively at dusk. In winter feeds more freely in open and during daylight. Small flocks may gather outside breeding season in feeding areas. Crouches when disturbed, often rising only when closely approached; characteristic zig-zag flight when flushed, frequently drops down to cover rapidly from considerable height. Food chiefly animal matter, including worms, molluscs and insects.
Nests on ground in tussock of grass or rushes, occasionally amongst heather.

Behaviour and feeding

Most easily confused with Jack Snipe (protected), which is much smaller and characteristically rises silently, very reluctantly (normally at walker's feet) and pitches down into cover after short flight. Woodcock somewhat similar to Snipe, but larger with stouter bill and heavier build.

Similar species

J	F	M	A	M	J	J	A	S	O	N	D
	31					12					

Shooting season

81

WOODCOCK

Scolopax rusticola
size: 34 cm (13½ in)

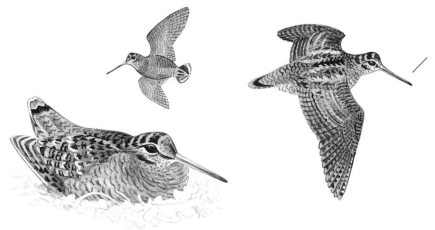

Field identification

Medium-sized, dark, round-winged wader with long straight bill. Plumage richly marked with browns, buff and black on upper-parts; under-parts light brown with fine dark-brown barring. Exceptionally well-camouflaged while at rest in woodland; in flight looks stout with short tail and long bill angled downwards. Sexes similar; young resemble adults.

Voice: virtually silent except during roding flights in spring and early summer.

Essentially a forest wader; breeding habitat typically dry, deciduous woodland with open, damp grassland areas for feeding; also in mixed broad-leaved and coniferous woodland and forestry plantations in northern parts of range. In winter retains affinity for woodland cover and open areas to feed. British breeding population largely sedentary, with some local movements. Autumn migrants from Scandinavia, Baltic states and western U.S.S.R. normally arrive in Britain mid-October to mid-November, overwintering mainly in western and southern districts; return migration mainly March to mid-April.

Habitat and distribution

Behaviour and feeding

Solitary and secretive. Rests during day in woodland ground vegetation. Flushed birds fly rapidly, dodging and weaving, and dropping quickly to cover again; rise with distinctive 'swish' of wings. Crepuscular, making regular flights to feeding grounds at dusk; also feeds in daylight in adverse weather conditions. Diet mainly animal material; earthworms of particular importance, also insects and larvae; uses long bill to probe deeply into soft ground to extract food.

Nests within woodland, often by trunk of tree or fallen branch, frequently in more open areas amongst bracken or brambles.

Similar species

Distinguished from Snipe by larger size, heavy appearance, thick bill, and to some extent by habitat preferences.

J	F	M	A	M	J	J	A	S	O	N	D
					ENGLAND & WALES				1		
	31				SCOTLAND			1			

Shooting season

82

PHEASANT

Phasianus colchicus
size: ♂ 76–89 cm (30–35 in)
 ♀ 53–64 cm (21–25 in)

Large gamebird; both sexes characterised by long, pointed tail. ♂ colouring very variable, but typically iridescent copper body plumage with glossy dark green head, scarlet wattle and white neck ring. ♀ about 30 per cent smaller than ♂, duller, mottled plumage tones varying from light buff to dark brown. Juvenile similar to adult ♀.
Voice: ♂ has a characteristic harsh, resonant crowing call; ♀ less vocal, but utters soft whistle when flushed.

Field identification

Mainly a lowland bird favouring wooded agricultural land, parkland, etc; wild population also frequents more open habitats, particularly marshes and occasionally moorland. Resident; extensively released into areas managed specifically for the benefit of this species.

Habitat and distribution

Very conspicuous, feeding in open, often in wet pastures and cultivated land adjacent to woodland. Tends to avoid flying unless forced; noisy take-off and strong flight with whirring wing-beats, flight usually direct and rapid but seldom sustained; will fly hard and fast for short period, then glide towards cover. Gregarious, often gather in flocks to feed; sexes frequently segregated. Normally roosts in trees; also takes to trees to avoid danger. Feeds on wide variety of plant and animal matter including seeds, fruits, green shoots, leaves, insects, earthworms, slugs, etc.
Ground-nesting usually in dense cover of tall grass, hedgerow, scrub, etc.

Behaviour and feeding

Large size and long tail are unmistakable characteristics; a wide range of colour variants occur; confusion can occur with feral birds of introduced species, particularly Golden and Lady Amherst's Pheasants.

Similar species

J	F	M	A	M	J	J	A	S	O	N	D
	1									1	

Shooting season

83

GREY PARTRIDGE

Perdix perdix
size: ♂ 31 cm (12 in)
     ♀ 29 cm (11½ in)

Field identification

Small, rotund gamebird with short wings and short, rufous tail. Sexes essentially similar, although ♂ slightly larger; both have characteristic orange-chestnut face, grey neck and under-parts and chestnut flanks; ♂ has conspicuous dark chestnut horse-shoe patch on lower breast, but this feature usually only poorly developed in ♀. Juvenile has orange or chestnut markings replaced by brown streaking.
Voice: usual call a loud, high-pitched, grating *kirr-ic*.

Habitat and distribution

Found principally in mixed farmland areas preferring extensive tracts of grassland with fringing hedgerows, rough grass or woodland cover, and some open ground. Mainly restricted to lowlands, but does occur up to 600 m (2000 ft) on moors and grass heaths adjacent to cultivated land. Frequently occurs in sand dunes, marshes and bogs.
Resident, with some local dispersal in autumn and winter months.

Behaviour and feeding

Almost exclusively ground-dwelling; normally walks or runs with rounded back and head low, but runs for cover with neck stretched up. Often crouches when alarmed; flies reluctantly, but when flushed flight strong and rapid with groups keeping well together.
Gregarious outside breeding season; with flock structure retained from early August to late winter. Pairs strongly territorial in breeding season.
Feeds largely on plant material; ♀♀ feeding young also take insects. Main components of diet are grass, leaves, cereals and clover, grain and other plant seeds.
Nests on ground in hedgerows, scrub or rough grassland; also in arable crops and cultivated grassland.

Similar species

Easily confused with slightly larger Red-legged Partridge; in particular, juveniles of the two species are very similar and difficult to separate. Quail (protected) is similar, but much smaller.

Shooting season

J	F	M	A	M	J	J	A	S	O	N	D

84

RED-LEGGED PARTRIDGE

Alectoris rufa
size: ♂ 34 cm (13½ in)
      ♀ 32 cm (13 in)

Field identification

Small, rotund gamebird with short wings and tail. Sexes have similar plumage, but ♂ slightly larger than ♀. Adult has distinctive long white eye-stripe, white throat and cheeks bordered black; chestnut, white and black barred flanks; red bill and legs; rest of plumage olive brown, grey and buff. Juvenile lacks distinctive head pattern and barred flanks.
Voice: call-note of ♂ a low, harsh *chucka chucka*; both sexes utter sharp, barking *kuk-kuk* when flushed.

Prefers dry, lowland areas, especially sandy heaths, chalk downs and open fields on light soils with low vegetation; occurs in a variety of habitats from open woodland to arable fields and pasture.
Introduced species; resident and largely sedentary.
Frequently released, and on an increasing scale in recent years.

Habitat and distribution

Normally walks or runs quickly over open terrain; may roost in trees as well as on ground. Flies very reluctantly, and coveys inclined to scatter when flushed from cover; flight typical of gamebird species. Gregarious outside breeding season; frequently in large flocks (over 50 birds). Solitary and in pairs during breeding period. Feeds largely on plant material – particularly grain, weed seeds, leaves, also roots (e.g. of sugar beet) and legumes; insects taken in late spring.
Nests on ground, usually sheltered by tussock of vegetation, bush, rocks, etc.

Behaviour and feeding

Easily confused with Grey Partridge, especially in flight. Quail (protected) is very much smaller, with duller plumage.

Similar species

J F M A M J J A S O N D

Shooting season

85

RED GROUSE

Lagopus lagopus scoticus
size: ♂ 36–39 cm (14–15½ in)
 ♀ 33–36 cm (13–14 in)

Field identification

Medium sized grouse characterised by rotund appearance, short wings; body plumage uniform dark rufous brown with darker wings and black rounded tail. Sexes closely similar, but ♀ more barred and a duller rufous colour. Adults appear greyer in winter, with white under-wing coverts and occasionally show white on flanks and belly. Juvenile generally like ♀.
Voice: call when flushed a loud, crowing *kok*.

Habitat and distribution

Primarily associated with open upland moorland and bogs dominated by heather; also in grass heaths with heather or other dwarf shrubs. Highest densities occur on well-managed heather moor on rich soils, giving optimum supply of food and shelter, mainly in eastern parts of range; poorer soils and preponderance of wet grassy heaths in west result in lower numbers. Resident, moves to lower ground and occasionally cultivated land in winter.

Behaviour and feeding

Basically a ground-dwelling bird, flies for short distances, usually close to ground unless driven higher. Flight strong and rapid, alternating between whirring wing-beats and gliding on decurved wings. Mainly gregarious outside breeding season; packs develop in early autumn as family parties disperse; normally up to 20 in a flock, occasionally more. ♂♂ become strongly territorial as winter progresses; non-territorial ♂♂ and ♀♀ remain in packs. Feeds almost exclusively on heather – particularly young shoots – throughout the year, but will take other plant material; insects may form a significant part of adult diet on blanket bogs and heather moors, and also taken by chicks at an early age.

Similar species

May be confused with ♀ Black Grouse; Ptarmigan always recognisable by smaller size and white wings and underparts.

Shooting season

J	F	M	A	M	J	J	A	S	O	N	D
						12				10	

86

BLACK GROUSE

Lyrurus tetrix (Tetrao tetrix)
size: ♂ 53 cm (21 in)
  ♀ 41–43 cm (16–17 in)

LEK DISPLAY POSTURE

Field identification

Medium-sized grouse. Sexes dissimilar. ♂ (Blackcock) plumage glossy blue-black with white wing-bar and curled, 'lyre-shaped' outer-tail feathers. ♀ (Greyhen) warm brown above, greyer and paler under-parts, mottled and barred with black throughout; forked tail. ♂ in eclipse plumage during autumn looks dingy, without characteristic lyre-shaped tail. Juveniles like small dull ♀.
Voice: ♂ usually silent away from lek; ♀ call-note a loud *tchuk*.

Habitat and distribution

Prefers margins of hilly moors, adjacent to woodlands (including conifer plantations), marshes, bogs, etc. Typical habitat includes scattered groups of trees with good cover, and clearings for display grounds. Resident; ♂ particularly sedentary; ♀♀ and juveniles seldom move great distances.

Behaviour and feeding

Flight strong and rapid, usually over short distances only; frequently higher than other moorland gamebirds, but low in cover; often circles both on take-off and landing. Gregarious throughout the year, especially ♂♂; large winter flocks can occur. Perches in trees, feeds in trees in winter; roosts and feeds on ground in summer. Feeds chiefly on plant material throughout year; summer diet includes leaves and shoots of ground plants, seeds, berries, fruits, etc, and some insects. Autumn and winter food primarily shoots and buds of birch and Scots pine.
Nests on ground in dense vegetation.

Similar species

♂ unmistakable, but ♀ may be confused with ♀ Red Grouse or Capercaillie. Confusing hybrids between Black Grouse and Capercaillie, Red Grouse and Pheasant occur.

J	F	M	A	M	J	J	A	S	O	N	D
							20			10	

Shooting season

87

PTARMIGAN

Lagopus mutus
size: 33–36 cm (13–14 in)

♂ SUMMER PLUMAGE   ♀ SUMMER PLUMAGE   ♂ WINTER PLUMAGE

Field identification

Small grouse; both ♂ and ♀ characterised by pure white wings and under-parts at all seasons. Three distinct seasonal plumage variations. In winter both sexes pure white except for black tail. ♂ in summer has dark greyish-brown and black mottled head, neck, flanks, upper breast and upper body and black tail; ♀ browner with tawny markings. ♂ in autumn replaces dark plumage with paler colours, tail remains black; ♀ darker. Juvenile like autumn ♀, but with pale brown wings and tail same colour as back.
Voice: call notes a low, grating croak and repeated cackling, often as alarm.

Habitat and distribution

Resident, restricted to arctic-alpine heaths. In summer found on high-level, open rocky or stony terrain with abundant bilberry and cranberry; generally above 600 m (2000 ft) in Cairngorms, at lower elevations further north; moves to lower ground in winter.

Behaviour and feeding

Frequently tame and easily approached; flies reluctantly, preferring to crouch and skulk, relying on immaculate camouflage to avoid detection. Flight typical of grouse family, but fast and will fly up and down steep slopes quickly and easily. Food is almost entirely plant matter, mainly shoots, leaves and berries of heathland plants, also buds, twigs and seeds of trees like birch where available. Diet varies with seasonal availability of foods; will dig through snow in winter to get to food plants.
Nests invariably on ground; generally in open, partly sheltered by rock or taller vegetation.

Similar species

Characteristic white wings and underbody, together with habitat preferences, easily distinguish Ptarmigan from other British grouse species.

Shooting season

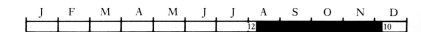

J F M A M J J A S O N D

88

CAPERCAILLIE

Tetrao urogallus
size: ♂ 84–90 cm (33–35 in)
       ♀ 58–64 cm (23–25 in)

♂

LEK DISPLAY POSTURE

Field identification

Very large grouse, with broad wings and rounded tail. ♂ 30 per cent larger than ♀; has overall dark plumage, body and head basically slate-grey and black with glossy blue-green breast; wings dark, rich brown; under-parts and tail marked with white. ♀ mottled with black, light grey and buff; dark brown upper-parts; characteristic rufous patch on breast contrasts with lighter under-parts. Juvenile generally similar to adult ♀.
Voice: ♂ silent outside breeding season; ♀ call note a loud, harsh *kcock*.

Inhabits chiefly mature coniferous woodland in upland areas; prefers mixture of fairly dense tree cover with thick undergrowth and open ground, especially moorland. Resident, but some local movements in winter, particularly by ♂♂.

Habitat and distribution

Behaviour and feeding

Usually ground-dwelling in summer and autumn; found in trees during winter. Breaks cover noisily, but flight quick, silent and usually brief; rarely flies above tree-top height. Typical gamebird flight, series of quick wing-beats alternating with glides on decurved wings, with neck extended. Food almost entirely vegetable material, varying with seasonal availability from shoots and buds of conifers from late autumn to early spring; including a range of grasses, clover, berries, seeds, etc during the rest of year.
Nests on ground in dense cover in forest, juniper scrub, occasionally in deep heather on open moor.

Adult ♂ unmistakable with characteristic dark plumage and large size. ♀ may be confused with ♀ Red or Black Grouse, but is much larger than both.

Similar species

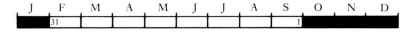

Shooting season

89

WOODPIGEON

Columba palumbus
size: 41 cm (16 in)

Field identification

Large, heavy pigeon, characterised by broad white band across wing seen readily in flight, and white patches on sides of neck. Sexes similar. Body plumage basically blue-grey, head and neck bluer than rest, flanks and underside paler; purple-green gloss to sides of neck. Young duller and lack white on wings and neck.
Voice: characteristic rhythmic, muffled *cooing* calls.

Chiefly occurs in cultivated areas and woodlands, but also in towns and cities. Feeds on farmland and uses trees and hedges to roost and nest. British breeding population mainly resident, with some local movements and emigration to north-west Europe; passage migrants and winter visitors from continent appear during October/November to
Habitat and distribution   March/April, mainly in eastern England.

Behaviour and feeding

Normally feeds during daylight on ground in open cultivated land or woodland glades; makes extensive use of agricultural crops particularly in autumn and winter, including spilt grain on stubble, turnips, brassicas, clover, etc; also takes buds, young leaves and flowers in spring. Gregarious outside breeding season; commonly feeds in very large flocks; roosts communally in woodland or hedgerows. When flushed rises with loud clatter of wings; strong flight usually direct and rapid. Nest site varies, but normally in woodland or hedgerow trees; occasionally building, rock ledges, rarely on ground.

Similar species

Confusion most likely with Stock Dove, Rock Dove and some domestic pigeons (all protected), but all are smaller and lack white wing and neck patches of Woodpigeon.

Shooting season

J	F	M	A	M	J	J	A	S	O	N	D

90

CROW

Corvus corone
size: 47 cm (18½ in)

CARRION CROW

HOODED CROW

Two races of this large corvid occur in the British Isles. The Carrion Crow (*C.c.corone*) has uniform sleek black plumage with a greenish or blue-purple gloss. The Hooded Crow (*C.c.cornix*) is black except for grey back and under-parts. Both have a heavy, dark brown bill, and square tail.
Voice: characteristic harsh, croaking *caw*.

Carrion Crow resident; population augmented by some winter immigrants from western Europe. Breeding range overlaps with Hooded Crow in north and east Scotland, where hybrids frequently occur. Hooded Crow resident in Scotland. Winter visitors from Baltic and Scandinavia occur mainly in eastern and central England during October/November to March/April. Found in a wide range of habitats from open moors and heaths, pasture and arable farmland, to parkland, wooded country, and coastlands.

Relatively solitary, and most frequently found singly or in pairs; very occasionally in small flocks, particularly at roosts. Flight usually direct, with slow deliberate wing-beats; rarely soars. Feeds chiefly on the ground in open country, walking or occasionally hopping while it forages. Crows are opportunist feeders and diet consequently differs with area and time of year; extremely varied food includes vegetable matter, carrion, small mammals, birds and eggs, amphibians, insects, etc.
Trees preferred for nesting, but will use low bushes, cliff ledges or on ground (usually on islets).

Hooded Crow unmistakable, although flight silhouette like Carrion Crow. Carrion Crow may be confused with Rook; other black corvids are the much larger Raven (protected), and smaller Chough (protected), both of which have very distinctive calls.

Field identification

Hooded Crow

Carrion Crow

Habitat and distribution

Behaviour and feeding

Similar species

J	F	M	A	M	J	J	A	S	O	N	D

Shooting season

91

ROOK

Corvus frugilegus
size: 46 cm (18 in)

Field identification

Large, black corvid with characteristic bare, white face-patch. Loose plumage around flanks gives 'shaggy trousers' appearance. Feathers have iridescent blue-purple or greenish gloss; slender, pointed bill is grey-black. Juvenile birds lack bare face patch, but characterised by loose flank feathers.
Voice: wide range of calls, but typically a fairly soft *kaw*.

Habitat and distribution

Chiefly in agricultural areas with suitable nesting trees. Forages in both pasture and cultivated land. Commonly close to small settlements, mainly in lowlands, and absent from urban areas. British birds resident; population supplemented by influx of winter immigrants from Scandinavia and central Europe, particularly to eastern Britain during October/November, departing late February/April.

Behaviour and feeding

Highly gregarious throughout the year. Normally encountered in small parties or flocks up to several hundred birds; in autumn and winter often roosts in very large numbers, frequently with Jackdaws.
Flight direct with regular, rapid wing-beats; sometimes glides and soars; flocks fly in loose formation. Walks easily, hopping occasionally. Feeds in open on the ground. Diet chiefly comprises vegetable matter, especially cereals, root crops, fruits, etc; animal food mostly gathered from grassland, primarily earthworms and leatherjackets obtained by probing the top layer of soil. Will also take a variety of invertebrates, carrion, small mammals, young birds and eggs.
Nests colonially, at traditional sites; normally in large trees, but not within extensive woodland areas; exceptionally on man-made structures. Most frequently uses beech, oak, elm, Scots pine and sycamore trees.

Similar species

May be confused with Carrion Crow. Some resemblance to Raven (protected) and Chough (protected), but these have distinctive call notes.

J	F	M	A	M	J	J	A	S	O	N	D

Shooting season

92

JACKDAW

Corvus monedula
size: 33 cm (13 in)

Small, dark corvid, characterised by grey nape and ear-coverts; under-parts dark grey, remaining plumage black. Distinctive pale grey eye, and short bill.
Voice: characteristic short, high-pitched, metallic *tchak*.

Field identification

Frequents a wide variety of relatively open habitats, from parkland and farmland to sea-cliffs, towers and old buildings, etc. Forages mainly in pasture land. British population generally sedentary, although some local movements and emigration to continent recorded. Winter immigrants from Europe appear during October/November to late February/April.

Habitat and distribution

Behaviour and feeding

Highly sociable corvid, often in large flocks and frequently associates with Rooks and Starlings when foraging in pastures. Moves on ground with quick, jerky walk; appears more alert and 'perky' than other corvids. Highly adaptable, omnivorous feeder; diet varies considerably with location and time of year. Spends much time feeding on surface insects in grassland; grain and wild plant seeds form an important part of vegetable matter eaten. Also takes legumes, earthworms, birds' eggs and nestlings, and carrion.
Usually nests in a hole in tree, building, rock face, etc; also constructs nest in trees.

Most likely confusion is with Chough (protected), but this species has distinctive flight and call-notes. Carrion and Hooded Crows, Raven (protected) and Rook all much larger and heavier than Jackdaw.

Similar species

J	F	M	A	M	J	J	A	S	O	N	D

Shooting season

93

MAGPIE

Pica pica
size: 46 cm (18 in)

Field identification

Medium-sized corvid, characterised by distinctive black and white plumage and long wedge-shaped tail (comprising 50 per cent of total length). Belly, flanks and scapulars white; rest of plumage black with blueish or greenish gloss. Sexes alike; juvenile a duller version of adult. *Voice*: an unmistakable harsh, loud, repetitive *chak-chak-chak*, easily heard at long range.

Habitat and distribution

Resident; chiefly in farmland and open country with hedges and trees, also urban parks, suburban gardens, etc.

Behaviour and feeding

Found singly, in pairs or small parties; some flocking occurs; in autumn and winter roosts. Flight direct, with rapid wing-beats. Feeds primarily on ground, walking or hopping, and usually close to cover, in woodland rides, adjacent to hedgerows, etc. Diet varied, including insects, carrion and vegetable matter, especially grain, berries, fruits, etc; predates nests containing eggs and young of small birds; takes small birds and mammals, and a variety of molluscs, earthworms, etc.
Prefers nesting in tall trees and bushes, commonly ash, oak, hawthorn, sycamore and alder; will use cliffs and crags if no suitable trees available; nest of sticks and earth frequently domed with thorny branches.

Similar species

Both adults and juveniles unmistakable, with distinctive plumage and voice.

J	F	M	A	M	J	J	A	S	O	N	D

Shooting season

JAY

Garrulus glandarius
size: 34 cm (13½ in)

Medium-sized corvid, characterised by white rump, black tail and white wing-patch conspicuous in flight. Body pinkish-brown; bright blue and black barred wing coverts; black and white erectile crown feathers; fairly long tail and short, rounded wings.
Voice: characteristic harsh, screeching call, very loud and detectable over long distances.

Primarily an inhabitant of oak woodlands, but found in variety of fairly open deciduous woodlands and coverts with good secondary growth, also mixed and coniferous woods, suburban gardens and parks, orchards, etc. British birds mainly resident, but local movements do occur; winter immigrants from Baltic and North Sea countries of continental Europe – often resulting from invasion movements rather than regular migratory movements – recorded mostly in south-east England.

Habitat and distribution

Rarely outside woods; moves in tree-canopy by jumping among branches; usually hops on the ground. Flies easily among trees, but in open flight appears weak and laboured with jerky, flapping action. Commonly in small parties or flocks outside breeding season.
Acorns predominate in autumn diet, and large numbers stored for winter feeding, hence close association with oak woodlands; other vegetable matter includes fruits, also grain and legumes; animal food includes young birds and (especially) eggs, and woodland insects.
Nests in trees, in more secluded parts of broadleaved or coniferous woodland.

Behaviour and feeding

Easily identified by voice and plumage characteristics plus habitat preference.

Similar species

J	F	M	A	M	J	J	A	S	O	N	D

Shooting season

95

BROWN HARE

MOUNTAIN HARE
(winter coat)

RABBIT

GREY SQUIRREL

BROWN (or FIELD) HARE

Lepus capensis
size: 50–68 cm (20–27 in)

Medium-sized mammal characterised by very long ears and long hind-legs. Ears have black tips; body colour yellowish- to reddish-brown in summer, becoming greyer in winter; upper tail is black.

Field identification

Primarily a lowland species; prefers open, relatively flat country, especially farmland, and also deciduous woodland. Extends to higher moors in some areas, where range overlaps with Mountain Hare. Introduced into Ireland.

Habitat and distribution

Mainly nocturnal and solitary. Moves very fast over the ground, leaping with legs fully stretched; frequently zig-zags, especially when bolting if disturbed from form. Feeds on a wide range of vegetation, including agricultural crops – and young forestry plantings.
Form may be in tall grass, scrub, woodland or open fields, and is normally well sheltered.

Behaviour and feeding

Resembles Mountain Hare and similar to, but much larger than, Rabbit.

Similar species

J	F	M	A	M	J	J	A	S	O	N	D

Shooting season

MOUNTAIN (or BLUE) HARE

Lepus timidus
size: 45–55 cm (18–22 in)

Medium-sized mammal characterised by long, black-tipped ears, and long hind-legs; tail lacks any black colouring. Body colour grey-brown to reddish-brown in summer; in winter largely white with black ear-tips, although not all individuals change colour, and in Ireland none attain white coat; during moult mixtures of white and grey-brown (or blueish-brown) occur.

Field identification

Mainly found in upland areas of Britain, but also on lower ground in Ireland (where it largely replaces the Brown Hare). Inhabits both open hillsides and mountain habitats, and woodlands, including forestry plantations.

Habitat and distribution

Behaviour and feeding

Normally fairly solitary, but may be found in small groups. Often active during daylight. Moves with leaping gait; when running tends to take a fairly direct line with little zig-zagging. Feeds on a wide variety of vegetation, including the bark and tops of young trees – occasionally inflicting serious damage to plantations.
Form normally amongst boulders or rocks, or grass tussocks.

Similar species

Mountain Hare (except in winter coat) closely resembles Brown Hare, and is similar to the much smaller Rabbit.

J   F   M   A   M   J   J   A   S   O   N   D

Shooting season

Oryctolagus cuniculus
size: 34–45 cm (13–18 in)

RABBIT

Field identification

Medium-sized mammal characterised by long ears and long hind-legs; short, woolly tail which is white on underside contrasting with black or brown-grey above. Body colour normally light brown, but wide range of colour varieties occur, notably black, fawn, white and silver-grey. (Shown in colour on p. 96.)

Found chiefly on light, sandy soils in open habitats – heaths, sand dunes, moorland, etc; also in woodland; generally not at higher elevations.
Local variations in population densities are largely controlled by outbreaks of the disease myxomatosis.

Habitat and distribution

Behaviour and feeding

Most active in evening, also feed during afternoon and at night. Moves with bounding gait; runs quickly, turning at sharp angles. Burrows extensively (only the doe actually excavates); lives colonially in warrens; occasionally lives above ground (especially young bucks). Feeds mainly on grass and other green herbage; frequently causes damage to farm and garden crops when local populations high in numbers; will gnaw tree bark, especially in winter and with a preference for saplings.
Capable of breeding throughout year, but mainly spring and early summer; young born in burrow dug away from main colony.

Similar species

Both Brown and Mountain Hares are larger, with longer ears and larger hind-legs.

J   F   M   A   M   J   J   A   S   O   N   D

Shooting season

GREY SQUIRREL

Sciurus carolinensis
size: 45–55 cm (17½–21½ in)

Medium-sized rodent. Characterised by long, bushy tail (nearly half total length); grey fur with some reddish and yellow tinges on back and flanks; and absence of prominent ear tufts. Under-parts white; gains silver-grey winter coat usually in late autumn, and shorter, brownish summer coat in spring. (Shown in colour on p. 96.)

Field identification

Introduced into Britain during late 19th and early 20th centuries; widespread by 1950s. Chiefly in deciduous woodland, particularly with oak, beech, chestnut and hazel. Also parkland, suburban gardens, etc; mainly in lowland areas; less frequently in coniferous woodland.

Habitat and distribution

Active during the day, particularly in early morning. Moves quickly on the ground with bounding gait. Varied diet includes grain, herbage and animal material. Plant components of diet dominated by nuts and other tree seed (including beech-mast), also leaves, buds, shoots, etc; strips bark to eat woody tissue (inflicting considerable damage in the process); animal material includes small birds, nestlings and eggs; also takes insects and fungi.

Behaviour and feeding

Resembles Red Squirrel (protected), although the latter is smaller, more lightly-built and mainly in coniferous woodland.

Similar species

J	F	M	A	M	J	J	A	S	O	N	D

Shooting season

FLOCK PATTERNS

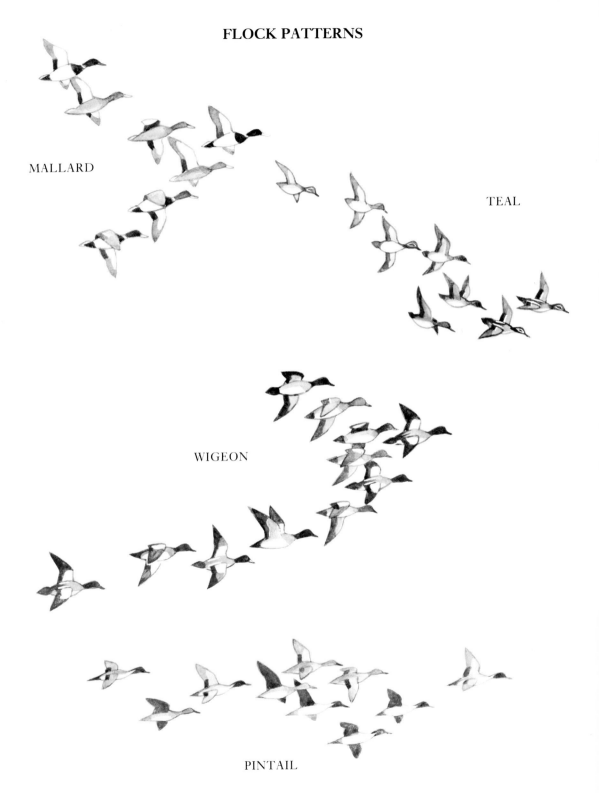

MALLARD

TEAL

WIGEON

PINTAIL

SHOVELER

GADWALL

TUFTED DUCK

POCHARD

GOLDENEYE

7   Roughshooting

The term 'roughshooting' embraces all forms of sporting shotgun shooting other than formal driven game shooting (see Chapter 8) and coastal duck, goose and wader shooting (see Chapter 9). It therefore includes the pursuit of game, pigeons, rabbit, hares, snipe and inland duck and geese

The pursuit of these quarry species can provide some of the most demanding and exciting sport to be found in this country; as with any form of sporting shooting, to be successful you must understand the habits of your quarry and these are explained briefly in the chapter on Quarry Identification.

Good roughshooting can be enjoyed on a small acreage of land, dependant upon the type and distribution of habitat. The form in which roughshooting takes place will largely be determined by the nature of the ground and by the quarry species being pursued.

WILDFOWL INLAND

Most rough shoots either provide or have the potential to provide an opportunity for inland duck shooting. If suitable ponds or wetlands do not exist then these can be created. The best opportunites for inland duck shooting come from either flighting a pond at dusk or by intercepting birds as they flight between their roosting and feeding areas. Good duck shooting can also be enjoyed when duck, particularly mallard, flight onto stubble fields during September and early October. This can be done at night, particularly for a few nights either side of the full moon, when there is sufficient moonlight and a light cloud covering against which the birds will be clearly silhouetted. If any area of the roughshooter's land floods after prolonged rainfall, they should keep an eye open for preened feathers and droppings; if these signs of duck occur, they should be prepared to take advantage of the fortuitous opportunity for flighting in that area.

The roughshooter's opportunity to pursue geese inland will be largely restricted to those which roost on reservoirs and lakes, however to lie in wait for them on their flight lines can be most exciting. The younger birds make excellent eating.

Snipe can provide some of the most testing shooting for the roughshooter and may be walked up or, most difficult of all, flighted as dusk as they come to a marshy spot to feed.

RABBIT SHOOTING

At one time rabbits were the mainstay of the roughshooter's bag, but the introduction of myxomatosis in the early 50s largely decimated the rabbit population. Whilst myxomatosis still occurs in certain areas, throughout a large part of the country the rabbit is on the increase.

Rabbits may be shot for sport in a number of ways. Often they are hunted out of hedgerows, patches of bracken and other cover with a dog. The method to be adopted will depend on the ability of the shooter to work his dog to the best advantage over a particular piece of ground. How rabbits can best be dealt with must be decided by those on the spot. Only the person with local knowledge gained from experience will know the place where rabbits will be most likely to be found, from which side of the hedgerows they are more likely to bolt into the open; and from what haven of safety, whether it be burrows or thick cover, they are likely to be flushed. Although most popularly known as a burrowing creature, rabbits will lie out for weeks in fields which provide some sort of cover such as thistles or roots. If rabbits are not walked up with a dog they can be stalked or ambushed as they emerge from their burrows to feed at evening time.

Ferreting is a particularly effective means of controlling the numbers of rabbits, but to go into details of ferreting is outside the scope of this book other than to say that no rabbit should ever be shot at the mouth of the hole as the ferret bringing up the rear will be endangered. rabbits should always be allowed to get a short distance from the burrow as a wounded one may well crawl down the hole – even a 'dead' rabbit can kick itself a couple of yards.

WOODPIGEON SHOOTING

The woodpigeon offers the roughshooter good sport, a cheap and tasty meal and a battle of wits throughout the year. The two main methods of shooting are roost shooting and decoying. The method chosen will depend on the time of year, the availability of food supplies and the type of countryside over which the roughshooter is operating. Roost shooting is primarily a winter activity and involves the shooter getting underneath the flightline of birds approaching the woodland or copse where they are going to roost at night or rest in the daytime.

For the majority of pigeon shooters, decoying as opposed to roost shooting is the main sport. Decoying can be enjoyed all the year round and depends only on the food supplies available. A good knowledge of the pigeons preferred diet and reconnaissance are two essential prerequisites for successful pigeon shooting.

GAME

Roughshooting for game is normally an activity undertaken by one or two shooters with a dog working hedgerows or ditches or may involve a larger party of guns walking-up. It is particularly important to always ensure that a shoot leader is appointed and that every member of the line retains their place in relation to the people on either side of them and that the line is kept straight.

A CODE OF CONDUCT FOR ROUGHSHOOTING

WHERE

Always ensure that you are authorised to shoot where you intend to go and that you know precisely where the shoot boundaries are located.

You should be aware of any public rights of way crossing the land over which you are shooting.

Always advise the owner and/or tenant in good time if you want to go shooting and check that it is convenient.

WHAT

Always confirm with the owner and tenant what quarry you may shoot.

An invitation to shoot over a piece of land will not always necessarily entail an invitation to shoot any quarry species.

It is important that you know precisely what species you may pursue.

Always ensure you have a valid game licence if shooting at game; carry it and your shotgun certificate with you.

EQUIPMENT

Always use suitably loaded cartridges for your quarry.

The combination of gun, cartridge, and choke is important, and will be influenced by personal preference.

The table is for standard 12-bore loads; smaller bore guns will have shorter effective ranges.

Shot size	Quarry	Maximum effective range
No 4/5	Ducks	35m (about 40yd)
No 5/6	Hares & Rabbit	35m (about 40yd)
No 6/7	Pigeon/Woodcock/Partridge/ Teal/Grouse/Pheasant	35m (about 40yd)
No 8	Snipe	35m (about 40yd)

IN THE FIELD

Always ensure your companions know your position and observe safe shooting angles.

If shooting in company, appoint a leader and always ensure that each member of the party knows the plan for the day.

Always identify your quarry and ensure that it is safe to shoot.

Make sure that you know what is beyond the target.

Always condemn unsporting shooting, that is at poor fliers and at birds out of range.

When engaged in vermin shooting or crop protection, shooting at poor fliers may be acceptable. Out-of-range shooting, whether at game or vermin species, is *not* acceptable.

Always seek to present your quarry as a sporting shot, giving it reasonable 'law'; this means that the flushing dog or ferret is not endangered.

'Law' in this context means to allow the quarry to gain sufficient distance from you to present both a safe and sporting shot.

Always respect the owner's property, crops, livestock and fences and follow the country code.

Open gates rather than climb them, and close them after you. Climb a secured gate at the hinged end. Never break rails, fences or hedges. Never walk in standing corn. Avoid disturbance to livestock; keep your dog under control.

Always be especially vigilant about keeping in a straight line when walking in thick cover or dead ground.

The going may be easy for you, but slow and difficult for your companions.

Never shoot at a bird just because it is in the range of your gun. It may present a more sporting shot for one of your companions.

Never shoot at partially obscured quarry.

Never be greedy. Do not shoot more than you can carry or really need. Do not overshoot; a viable breeding stock must be left on the ground at the end of the season.

Crop protection may be an exception.

If a bird is shot and falls over the boundary, it is proper to seek permission to retrieve it.

Good relationships with sporting 'neighbours' are very important.

Never take your gun with you unless you have been authorised.

Never leave litter, take your empty cartridge cases home.

If you have been shooting from a hide, make sure that the area is left in such a way that no one can tell that you have been there.

AT THE END OF THE DAY
Always ensure that you have collected up all your equipment.

Always leave the place tidy.

It is courteous to thank the owner or occupier and to offer him something from the bag.

Always attend to your dog before yourself.

If the journey home is a long one, your dog may appreciate a drink before you leave.

Always inspect your dog for thorns and cuts.

Treat them promptly.

Always take your quarry from the game bag as soon as possible. Store it in a cool fly-proof place. Do not waste it.

Always clean your gun before putting it away; check it over for faults which may need attention.

Have any faults attended to immediately.

Walking up

Formal Driven Game Shooting

Formal driven game shooting is a highly organised aspect of the sport of shooting in which 'Game' birds are driven by beaters over or towards a line of standing guns.

Gamebirds, as defined by the Game Act 1831, are pheasants, partridges, grouse, ptarmigan and black grouse.

Historically, game was shot by 'walking up' and shooting birds as they flew away, but in the mid-to-late 1800s, coinciding with the general introduction of breech loaders, a change occurred and the guns stood whilst the birds were driven over them by beaters. This became a very institutionalised and formal aspect of the sport around which a strict code of conduct, or etiquette, has now evolved.

Ptarmigan are normally only shot when walking up, and are therefore outside the scope of this chapter.

WHERE

Shooting rights over any piece of land are always legally held by someone.

There are many ways of organising the management of game shooting rights. The most common are:

1. The landowner may retain the game shooting rights and organise the shooting for the benefit of themselves and their guests.

2. The landowner may retain the shooting rights, but invite a limited number of outside guns to each pay a set sum of money to have a gun in the shoot for one season. This system helps the shoot owner to defray the costs of running the shoot.

3. The landowner may retain the shooting rights and each season sell a number of shooting days to outside guns who each pay for one day's shooting. This is another way of defraying costs.

4. The landowner may lease the game-shooting rights to an individual who then becomes responsible for the financing and running of the shooting in any way he wishes.

5. The landowner may lease the shooting rights to a 'syndicate' of guns who take on the full responsibility of financing and organising the shooting in any way they wish.

6. An individual or a group of people or 'Company' (i.e. a sporting agency) may buy the shooting rights over one or more parcels of land in perpetuity or for a set period of time, and run the shooting in any way they wish.

7. A sporting agency may lease the shooting rights and 'sell' shooting days to outside guns.

Most formal shoots vary from about 400 up to several thousand acres in size.

As will be seen from the above, there is no set pattern as to how the management of shooting rights is organised, it being up to the owner or the lessee of the shooting rights to decide what system suits him best.

WHEN

The open and close seasons for game shooting are defined by the Game Act 1831. The open seasons are:

SHOOTING SEASONS

England, Wales and Scotland

Pheasant	1 October–1 February inclusive
Partridge	1 September–1 February inclusive
Grouse/Ptarmigan	12 August–10 December inclusive
Blackgame	20 August–10 December inclusive
Snipe*	12 August–31 January inclusive
Woodcock*	1 October–31 January inclusive (England and Wales)
	1 September–31 January inclusive (Scotland)

*Requires a Game Licence, but is not 'Game' within the meaning of the Game Act 1831.

NORTHERN IRELAND

The shooting seasons and quarry species differ from those in England, Wales and Scotland. They are subject to yearly change (for example, Partridge and hen Pheasants are currently protected).

At the peg

CODE OF PRACTICE

Always remember your responsibility to safeguard your quarry and its environment for future generations.

The quality of the sport is more important than pure numbers, and one should endeavour to produce truly sporting shots.

Always remember that others will judge the sport by your behaviour and that of your companions.

Always ensure you have made adequate provision for finding lost game, either by inviting your guests to use their own gundogs, or by arranging for an appropriate number of 'pickers-up'.

Always make provision for the proper treatment of shot game by ensuring that it is hung up in the 'game cart' to cool quickly, kept clean, dry and stored in a cool flyproof larder.

Always ensure that if transport is needed between drives for guns and beaters, that it is adequate for the purpose and safe.

It is good management to see that both guns and beaters have somewhere dry to eat their lunch and that water is available for gundogs.

The arrangements for the day and the marking out of the stands should be agreed with the keeper well beforehand.

The organisation of the day is your responsibility: make sure everybody knows what is expected of them.

THE GUEST'S OBLIGATIONS

Always reply promptly to an invitation to shoot.

Make sure you know whether you are expected to take your dog and your lunch; also ensure that you know the time and place to meet.

Always remember that it is the sportsman's responsibility to understand the laws relating to his sport; in particular to be able to recognise his quarry and know when and where he may shoot.

Always arrive punctually.

Always wear a hat, sensible footwear and suitable clothing to suit your surroundings.

Always keep your gun in its cover between drives and while travelling in vehicles.

Always go to your stand quickly and quietly and check where the other guns are placed.

Acknowledge the gun on either side of you, or any 'stops' or pickers-up by raising your hat or hand, but not by calling out.

A 'stop' is someone who is positioned in order to stop game running or breaking out to the side of the drive.

Always check the direction the beaters will come from, the position of stops and where the pickers-up are placed.

Always check if there is any agricultural work in progress in your vicinity.

Always remain quiet at your peg, and do not move from where you were placed, unless so instructed by your host.

Always condemn unsporting shooting, i.e. at poor flyers and birds out of range.

Always 'mark' all game shot and collect those near your peg at the end of the drive.

Either use your own dog, or tell a picker-up the numbers and whereabouts of lost or wounded game so that they can be quickly brought to hand and despatched. A sharp knock on the head with a suitably heavy stick or priest is recommended.

Always ask your host what game is to be shot, and the position regarding ground game and vermin.

Always ask how many guns are shooting and, if you draw for a number, how the system works.

At most shoots, pegs will be numbered 1–8; No 1 is usually on the right and No 8 on the left of the drive. The normal practice is to move up two numbers for each consecutive drive. Make sure you know what number peg you should be at for each drive.

Always ensure you have a valid game licence, and carry it and your shotgun certificate with you.

A responsible shot will have Third Party Liability Insurance cover. B.A.S.C. membership provides this.

Never bring a guest with you without first confirming that you may.

Never be afraid to seek advice on any aspect relating to the conduct of the day.

Never take long shots, or shoot at partially obscured game.

Never load your gun until the drive commences and unload as soon as it is finished.

If shooting with a pair of guns, make sure you and your loader have practised the method of changing guns. The person passing the gun will hold it in his right hand at the grip with the barrels pointing upwards; the person receiving the gun will take it in his left hand by the fore-end. The safety catch should be on 'safe' throughout.

Never shoot between drives.

Never shoot low in front when the beaters are approaching.

Never let excitement cloud your judgement.

Never shoot behind without first taking the gun from your shoulder, keeping the barrels pointing vertically.

Never be greedy. Just because a bird is in range of your gun does not necessarily make it yours; it may produce a more sporting shot for one of your companions.

GUNS AND CARTRIDGES

Always use suitably loaded cartridges for your quarry.

The combination of gun, cartridge and choke is important, and will be influenced by personal preference.

Shot Size	Quarry	Maximum Effective Range
No 6/7	Grouse Partridge Pheasant Woodcock	35m (about 40yd)

Remember that relatively little choke is needed for game shooting. The recommendations are for standard 12-bore loads; smaller bore guns will have shorter effective ranges.

Always thank the keepers, beaters and pickers-up as it is largely their efforts which have provided your sport.

It is customary always to tip the head keeper, but if in doubt check with your host.

Always take care of any game which you have been given. Do not waste it.

Always ensure that you have collected up all your equipment.

Always thank your host for your days sport, and as an extra courtesy write and thank him later.

Always feed and water your dog before yourself and check him over for thorns and cuts.

Clean your gun, and check it for faults which may need rectifying.

Have any faults attended to immediately by a competent gunsmith.

For many centuries duck, goose and wader shooting has been part of life on estuaries around our coast. The participant was and still is referred to as a wildfowler and he continues to follow old traditions established by professional wildfowlers. Wildfowling is purely a sport now, with sportsmen in pursuit of a restricted number of the edible quarry species. Normally the sportsman is on foot, but in some circumstances boats are used. It is a thoroughly modern recreation; it rewards the correct use of ancient skills as well as the understanding of nature. It requires toughness and preseverance. It can provide comradeship and a source of food.

Purists will argue that true wildfowling is strictly a coastal activity, taking place below the high-water mark – that is, on the foreshore around the coast. However, duck and goose flighting does take place inland on marshes, lakes and specifically managed flight-ponds and many mallard are reared, released and shot on shoots throughout the country.

England, Wales and Northern Ireland: definition of foreshore

In England, Wales and Northern Ireland the traditional place for wildfowling is that part of the seashore which is more often than not covered by the flux and reflux of the four oridinary tides occurring midway between spring and neap tides. This is called the foreshore and much of it is in Crown ownership or subject to control by the holders of regulating leases from the Crown Estate Commissioners. The remaining areas are generally in private hands.

Since 1968 through an agreement between the Crown Estate and BASC, BASC members have been allowed the privilege to continue wildfowling on Crown Estate foreshore where the sporting rights remain in the hands of the Crown. In more recent years the Crown Estate have been encouraging BASC affiliated wildfowling clubs to take leases of sporting rights on Crown Estate foreshore and BASC has actively assisted its clubs in this process. This has allowed for increased management of the foreshore and greater security for shooting. There are now very few areas available under the agreement not managed by clubs and all important areas will be under management by 2001 by which time the general agreement will have been phased out. Wildfowlers seeking foreshore wildfowling can obtain information on local wildfowling clubs from BASC.

Scotland: definition of foreshore

In Scotland the foreshore is defined slightly differently as the area between high- and low-water marks of ordinary spring tides. In Scotland, whether the ownership pertains to the Crown or a private individual, the Crown retains in trust for the public certain rights, including recreation, on the foreshore (except on Orkney and the Shetlands) by virtue of which members of the public may engage in wildfowling. This public right may only be taken away by statute as, for example, by the establishment of nature reserves under the National Parks and Access to the Countryside Acts 1949, by declaration of areas of special protection under the Wildlife and Countryside Act 1981, or the establishment of country parks under the Countryside (Scotland) Act 1967 and Countryside Act 1968. As before, the onus is on the wildfowler to establish whether such statutory controls exist.

UNDERSTANDING THE HABITS OF YOUR QUARRY

Ducks

Generally ducks feed by night, flighting between feeding and resting places at dawn and dusk. On the foreshore ducks will also feed in daylight and their habits will be affected by the tide. The stronger the tide, the rougher the water and the more marked will be the movement of birds.

Geese

Geese feed by day, flighting between the feeding and resting places at dawn and dusk. On moonlit nights, however, some species, in particular Pinkfooted and White-fronted geese, will flight back to their feeding grounds from their roost. The roost may be a large expanse of inland water or on the open shore or sea. During the few nights around full moon they may even remain on the feeding grounds throughout the whole period.

Waders

Movement of wading birds is largely based on the tides, feeding as they do almost exclusively on the intertidal zone. Golden Plover is the only quarry wader species (other than Snipe and Woodcock) and they regularly flight inland and feed on pastures.

Coastal Shooting

Coastal shooting provides immense variety; when high winds and rough weather prevail, tide flighting or decoying Wigeon on the flashes, which often remain after the tide has ebbed, can provide some of the season's most exciting sport. Wigeon flight well under the moon, too.

Successful wildfowlers rarely achieve satisfactory bags without acquiring a detailed knowledge of local conditions. This includes information about the prevailing and expected weather, the tides and their combined effect on the flighting and feeding habits of the birds. Such observations can be every bit as fascinating as the actual shooting. Binoculars are an essential piece of equipment.

At the beginning of the season, which starts on 1 September, the foreshore shooter will expect to see wildfowl and waders which have bred in Britain. At dawn and dusk Mallard and Teal will establish flight lines to and from their inland feeding grounds.

At this time, since many Mallard will be feeding on corn stubbles, the wildfowler will endeavour to place himself strategically where he can intercept their flight. During these early weeks of the season the birds, such as barley-fed Mallard, are at their best for eating.

By October the migratory duck and geese will have started to arrive in large numbers. Most estuaries are visited by small parties of migratory Mallard, Wigeon, Teal and Pintail to supplement the resident populations of Mallard and Teal.

Once wintry weather prevails, the wildfowler is in his element; the best results are often achieved when conditions are at their worst. Strong winds in particular keep the wildfowl on the move in an effort to find shelter, and when the fresh inland marshes freeze up, wildfowl are forced to move to more open coastal areas.

Under prolonged and extreme wintry weather, hungry birds rapidly lose body condition and become more approachable – thus no longer a worthy quarry. At such times the true sportsman has no need to be told when to use restraint, but the Wildlife and Countryside Act 1981 empowers the Secretary of State to invoke a statutory ban on wildfowling until the conditions have improved and the birds fully recovered.

Setting out decoys

THE PRINCIPLES OF WILDFOWLING

Always know where you can shoot by understanding the definition of foreshore in the area where you intend to shoot.

You must understand the definition of foreshore as given on page 113.

Always know what you can shoot and be capable of identifying common quarry that you intend to shoot.

Those who shoot on the foreshore can only legally take the birds listed in Schedule 2 Part I of the *Wildlife and Countryside Act 1981* unless otherwise authorised. Schedule 2 Part I lists those wild birds which may legally be shot during the open season. (See Appendix 4 on page 139.)

Schedule 2 Part II refers to those birds which may be killed or taken at any time by authorised persons; you should be aware that some bye-laws, for example on nature reserves, do not include the shooting of birds in Schedule 2 Part II.

WILDFOWL SEASONS

Always know when you can shoot the quarry you intend to pursue.

England, Scotland and Wales
Inland: 1 September – 31 January inc.
Below the mean high-water mark of ordinary spring tides: 1 September – 20 February inc.
NB Geese and Ducks only, *not* Waders, after 31 January.

Northern Ireland
The shooting seasons and quarry species differ from those in England, Scotland and Wales and are subject to yearly change; for example, Canada Geese are currently protected. There is no shooting on the foreshore after 31 January and night shooting is prohibited.

The shooting of wildfowl on Sunday is illegal in some areas.

Counties and County Boroughs in England and Wales in which there is no Sunday shooting of Schedule 2 Part I. Birds: Anglesey, Brecknock, Caernarvon, Cardigan, Carmarthen, Cornwall, Denbigh, Devon, Doncaster, Glamorgan, Great

Yarmouth, Isle of Ely, Leeds, Merioneth, Norfolk, Pembroke, Somerset, Yorkshire (North Riding), Yorkshire (West Riding).

NB The Counties referred to are those which were in existence before local government re-organisation in the early 1970s. It is the sportsman's responsibility to check whether or not Sunday shooting is allowed in the area he wishes to wildfowl.

There is no shooting of wildfowl in Scotland on Sundays or Christmas Day.

Never shoot from a mechanically propelled boat.

It is illegal to shoot from a mechanically propelled boat in the immediate pursuit of wildfowl. The prudent wildfowler will, therefore, dispense with the engine altogether.

COASTAL SHOOTING

Guns and Cartridges

Always choose a gun that is suitable for the type of shooting you intend to pursue.

A double-barrelled 12-bore is a suitable all round shotgun. If your fieldcraft is good, you will be successful with the standard 65mm (2½in) cartridge (correctly loaded). Traditionally, wildfowlers prefer a 75mm (3in) chambered gun which enables them to shoot heavier shot more effectively. Big bore guns, i.e. 10, 8 and 4 bores, although capable of handling big shot very effectively can be cumbersome and a burden. Choke only marginally increases effective range and is no excuse for attempting out-of-range shots.

The use of any gun or rifle firing a single bullet for the purpose of killing wildfowl, whilst not prohibited by law, is not an accepted sporting practice, and is discouraged by BASC for its members. The Wildlife and Countryside Act 1981 prohibits the use of automatic and semi-automatic shotguns for wildfowling unless they are restricted to fire not more than three cartridges in succession without reloading.

117

Always choose a cartridge suitable for the type of shooting you intend to pursue.

The following shot sizes are recommended:

Shot Size	Quarry	Maximum effective range
No 4/5	Ducks	35m (about 40yd)
No 6	Teal/	
	Waders	35m (about 40yd)
BB No 1		
or No 3	Geese	35m (about 40yd)

The cartridge must also be compatible with the gun you are using; see proofing on page 31.

Please note some lead free shot is less dense than lead and may necessitate going up one or two sizes in shot size. Steel is an example of one such material.

PLANNING

Always plan your wildfowling outings very carefully.

When you go on the foreshore for the first time, go in daylight with someone who knows the area and can point out marsh boundaries and any inherent dangers which occur.

When wildfowling away from home it is courteous to make contact with the Secretaries of any local wildfowling clubs to ensure you do not inadvertently encroach on private ground.

Always tell someone where and when you are going wildfowling.

Do not forget to tell them you have returned safely.

Always make sure you know of local rules and restrictions.

You should be particularly aware of those rules that may be operating in a controlled shooting area. It is the sportsman's responsibility to find out about them before going onto a marsh.

Always consult Tide Tables before going on the marsh.

Always avoid the more distant parts of the marsh when a big tide is expected.

Remember that the figures stated will be altered by the prevailing weather conditions. Winds particularly can affect tide levels. Remember, if British Summer Time is in force, to make the necessary correction to your Tide Table.

EQUIPMENT

Always pay particular attention to equipment; check its condition before going wildfowling.

The following items of equipment are recommended:

Waterproof wristwatch – essential for judging the state of the tide;

Waterproof torch – but remember torch flashing is *only* justified in an emergency;

Binoculars – useful for identification purposes;

Six-foot wading pole – assists walking on the marsh, useful for sounding gutters and crossing places;

Pocket compass – essential in order to be able to work out direction to your chosen point and for establishing a safe return route, especially in mist or fog.

Pull-through – a means of cleaning barrels if snow or mud enters them. A piece of rag on a cord is adequate.

If you are going out all day, carry some food and a thermos containing a hot drink.

Make sure you take necessary documents with you:

Shotgun Certificate

Game Licence (if you intend to shoot Snipe or Woodcock)

Local Permit (if applicable).

Wear comfortable, inconspicuous, warm, waterproof clothing. Waders are normally recommended.

Always take a large canvas bag – it is often useful to sit on.

If you are using a punt or boat, make sure that it is seaworthy and that you have paddles/oars, anchor, baler, life-jacket and emergency flares.

A responsible shot will have public liability insurance cover, but the best insurance is to follow BASC Shotgun Safety Code.

Remember a marsh can be spoilt by continual human disturbance: you need not be shooting to cause a disturbance.

BEHAVIOUR ON THE MARSH

Always remember that the wildfowlers' main quarry – wild geese and ducks – are largely migrants and as such are an internationally shared resource; we have a responsibility to safeguard them and their environment.

Always remember that others judge the sport of wildfowling by your behaviour.

One foolish or irresponsible act brings the whole sport into disrepute. Do not disturb the locality or other sportsmen by making a noise, banging car doors when arriving early in the morning or leaving late at night.

Never arrive late, or depart early, in relation to flight times (which will vary according to tides, winds, etc.); and do not disturb the shooting of those who have taken the trouble to get into position in good time.

Do not shoot in the immediate vicinity of houses adjoining the shore.

Make sure you are well hidden: camouflage yourself to suit your surroundings.

Look through your gun barrels to make sure they are clear whenever an obstruction may have entered.

Range-judging when wildfowling is particularly difficult as the flight develops; don't spoil it by shooting too early at out-of-range birds.

Take care to recognise legal quarry: if in doubt, don't shoot.

Never leave cartridge cases or unsightly pit-holes on the marsh.

Never try to be clever waiting for the last moment to leave the marsh when the incoming tide is approaching. Channels fill quickly and in a very short time they become a torrent.

Always condemn unsporting shooting i.e. at poor fliers and at birds out of range.

Always be accompanied by a gundog.

A dog is essential for tide shooting and picking-up after dark, but keep it under control at all times.

Dogging the tideline will often recover lost birds.

Try and make your dog comfortable; if you sit on your game bag, make sure that he has a dry seat.

Send your dog to retrieve birds as they are shot. The tide may carry the birds away.

Always mark wounded quarry and ensure that it is picked up and humanely despatched as soon as possible.

A sharp knock on the head with a suitably heavy stick or priest is most effective.

ON LEAVING THE MARSH

Always consider the needs of your dog before your own

He may be cold and wet: dry him and provide him with a dog blanket or bedding to lie on.

Always take care of your quarry.

Ensure that it is hung in a cool, dry place. Do not waste it.

Always pay special attention to cleaning your gun.

Mud and saltwater will quickly corrode it. Check it for faults which may need rectifying.

Whatever form of shooting you engage in, whether it be rough-shooting, formal driven game shooting or coastal wildfowling, your enjoyment of the sport will be increased by the presence of a well trained gundog. There are four very sound reasons why BASC strongly recommends that anyone who goes shooting should be accompanied by a trained and competent gundog. A dog can find, retrieve and bring to hand quarry which falls into thick cover or into or across water and which therefore could not be picked up by the shooter. A gundog is also able to find and retrieve game which is only wounded. A gundog is able to cover ground and search undergrowth which the shooter is not able to and thus increases the chances of finding and flushing quarry. Equally important is the fact that a dog is a wonderful companion and will make a shooting day more varied, interesting and enjoyable.

GUNDOGS

All breeds of gundogs have their supporters and good and bad examples of all breeds can be seen in the shooting field. It does not really matter which breed of gundog you choose, but the following is an outline of the various breeds and the manner in which they are generally used.

RETRIEVERS

The primary function of Retrievers is to search for and retrieve dead or wounded quarry. Retrievers are frequently used by game shooters who stand at pegs or by pickers-up on formal driven game shoots. Due to the nature of the coat of the Labrador Retriever, it is a good dog for the wildfowler as it does not suffer from the cold to any great extent. Of the four Retriever breeds the black Labrador is the most common
The breeds in this groups are:

The Curly-coated Retriever

The Flatcoated Retriever

The Labrador Retriever   The Golden Retriever

Spaniels are used primarily for questing – that is to hunt or search ground and cover in order to flush quarry. By far the most popular is the English Springer Spaniel which can be either liver and white, black and white or a tricolour combination of black, liver and white.

The breeds in this group are:

The English Springer Spaniel

The Welsh Springer Spaniel

The Cocker Spaniel

The Sussex Spaniel

The Field Spaniel

The Clumber Spaniel

The Irish Water Spaniel

POINTERS AND SETTERS · The purpose of Pointers and Setters is to range in front of the gun or guns and to indicate the presence of quarry by adopting a rigid pose. This is called pointing.

The breeds in this group are:

The English Pointer

The English Setter

The Gordon Setter

The Irish Setter

ALL-PURPOSE GUNDOGS · The purpose of these breeds is to hunt, point, flush and retrieve. The breeds in this group are:

The German Short-haired Pointer

The Vizsla

The Weimeraner

The Large Munsterlander

Having established the various breeds which are normally used for different purposes, it must be stressed that it is up to the individual to decide which breed is most suitable for his type of shooting and circumstances.

ACQUIRING A GUNDOG

If you consider your gun to be the most important piece of equipment, then certainly your dog comes a close second. You must therefore give great care and consideration to the acquisition of a gundog.

You may decide to buy a puppy, usually between 8 and 12 weeks old; or you may decide to buy a fully trained adult dog or a dog which is only partly trained. The choice is up to the individual and depends upon various circumstances. It is not our intention within this chapter to even begin to explain to you how to set about training a gundog, but simply to make you aware of a number of basic points which you should consider even before acquiring one. You must obviously give thought to kennelling, feeding, diet, cost and the dog's need for exercise. All gundogs need to be fit: they require a considerable amount of regular exercise.

BASIC TRAINING OF GUNDOGS

Should you decide to acquire a puppy, you will also have to decide whether or not you will train it yourself or whether you will send it away to be trained. If you decide to train the dog yourself, work out a programme or follow the guidelines as laid down in a recommended book, such as *Know Your Gundog Training* by Roy Jordan.

Briefly, basic training should consist of sitting to command, walking to heel, stopping immediately on command, stopping and sitting to shot, coming back when called, understanding the command 'No', observing directional hand signals, being steady to moving quarry and dropping to flush. Never take an untrained dog into the shooting field as it will spoil the enjoyment of all.

DOG HANDLING IN THE FIELD

When out shooting with your dog there is a certain code of conduct which you should follow at all times:

Always carry a lead and use it whenever you have to walk your dog along a road.

Always keep your dog under control at all times and do not allow it to disturb livestock.

Always check with your host that you can take your dog with you when invited out shooting. If your host has organised pickers-up, your dog may not be welcome.

Always see to your dog's comfort before looking after yourself after a day's shooting. If you have to travel, make sure that its bed in the car is warm. When you get home, check it for thorns and cuts and give any treatment necessary.

Always rub your dog down with a sack or towel if it is wet after a day's shooting. See that its kennel is dry and draughtproof with a comfortable bed.

Never allow your dog to pick up quarry shot by another shooter except with his agreement. This is important as shooters must keep a count of how many birds they have down at any one time in order to make sure that every bird which is shot is retrieved.
A shooter may also wish his own dog to retrieve a bird which he has shot.

Never allow your dog to take dead or wounded quarry from another dog.

Never allow your dog to fight with other dogs or to worry bitches.

Never take a bitch which is in season into the company of other dogs in the field.

Never have a collar on your dog when it is working. Dogs have been hung by collars when going over banks, down gullies and over walls. Dogs have also been drowned when a branch or wire under water has caught on a collar.

Never attach your dog's lead to yourself when shooting.

Never send your dog over the boundary of your shoot unless you have permission to do so.

Never overtire your dog.

If your dog has had a very hard morning, it is much better to leave it in the car after lunch or make it walk to heel in the afternoon, rather than overtire it.

A keen and alert pupil sits on command.

Following directional hand signals.

Steadiness in company is essential.

Training should be enjoyable – for man and dog.

Gamekeeping

Anyone who actually takes part in game shooting and/or rough-shooting should understand the work of a gamekeeper, and appreciate their role in habitat and game management.

THE ROLE OF THE GAMEKEEPER

A gamekeeper is employed on a shoot to look after and encourage the game population. This is done by either protecting the wild stock, and thus allowing them to breed, or by rearing and releasing game birds thus augmenting the overall game population.

IN HABITAT CREATION
AND MANAGEMENT

It is necessary to create a suitable environment for a healthy game population. The gamekeeper achieves this by planting hedges, spinneys and game crops on the shoot. These provide food, nesting cover and shelter for game birds and thus the 'carrying capacity' of the shoot is increased.

IN CONSERVATION

A keepered environment sustains a greater overall wildlife population than an unkeepered environment. The reason for this is that the gamekeeper, whilst looking after the interests of the game population by creating or protecting existing habitat and killing vermin which predate upon game, is providing habitat and protected surroundings for songbirds, wild animals and plants. In this way a valuable contribution to the conservation of the countryside is made.

THE NEED TO
SUPPLEMENT WILD
GAMEBIRD STOCKS

Wild gamebird populations may need to be supplemented by rearing and releasing additional stocks. On a shoot where there are not large stocks of gamebirds (pheasants, grey and red-legged partridges) and duck to provide sport for the guns, then it is the gamekeeper's job to rear and release game to supplement the wild population.

MEANS OF INCREASING
THE STOCK OF
GAMEBIRDS

There are four main ways of doing this:

*1 Releasing from egg
production to poult*

Game birds are caught and penned before the end of the shooting season (December–January). The following spring these captive birds produce eggs which are incubated either artificially in incubators or under broody hens. The resulting chicks are reared by the gamekeeper and released into the wild at 6–8 weeks old. The release programme is a gradual process, thus allowing the young gamebirds to acclimatise to their new surroundings.

2 Releasing from purchased eggs to poult stage	Eggs are brought from a reputable game farm which sells large numbers of gamebird eggs, chicks and poults (young gamebirds). These eggs are incubated; the chicks are reared by the gamekeeper and then released on to the shoot at 6–8 weeks old.
3 Releasing from purchased chick to poult stage	Day-old gamebird chicks are bought from a game farm, the chicks are reared and released onto the shoot by the gamekeeper.
4 Releasing bought in poults	6–8 weeks old poults are purchased from a game farm and released gradually onto the shoot.
VERMIN	The control of both ground and avian predators is of utmost importance if gamebirds are to thrive on a shoot. If the vermin population is not kept in check, then nesting gamebirds and recently released poults would have little chance of survival. So it is the gamekeeper's job to control vermin.
	Predators can be defined as animals which predate upon eggs, chicks, poults and adult gamebirds, and can be divided into two categories:
1 Ground Predators:	These are animals which predate at times upon game and live and breed at ground level. These include: fox, feral, cat, mink, stoat, weasel and brown rat.
2 Avian Predators:	These are birds which often predate upon gamebirds eggs and chicks and include: carrion crow, hooded crow, rook, jackdaw, magpie, jay, greater black-backed gull and lesser black-backed gull.
	There are other avian predators which are protected by the Wildlife and Countryside Act 1981 (see page 138) and should not be killed.
METHODS OF VERMIN CONTROL	There are five main methods of vermin control that are available to a gamekeeper:
1 Shooting	The gamekeeper usually carries a shotgun when working on the shoot and often has the chance to shoot both ground and avian predators.
2 Trapping – Tunnel Traps	Artificial tunnels are placed at strategic points round the estate. A Fenn Mk IV Spring Trap or similar is placed, and set, in each of these tunnels. Ground predators (except foxes, feral cats) hunting for food will investigate these tunnels and be caught in the trap.
3 Trapping – Cage Traps	Cage traps of different varieties will catch all avian and ground predators. They have either to be baited with food, or camouflaged to look like a natural tunnel, to entice the vermin to enter.

4 Snaring	The use of free-running snares, set correctly according to the BASC Snaring Code of Practice, is the most efficient way of controlling the number of foxes on a shoot.
5 Poison	The correct use of legally prescribed poison is a very efficient way of controlling certain vermin, such as a rat infestation on a shoot.
SHOOT DAY MANAGEMENT	It is a gamekeeper's responsibility to ensure that everything runs smoothly on a shoot day. He is responsible for organising the following:
1 Guns	Making sure that numbered pegs are correctly positioned at each drive (see Chapter 8: Game Shooting).
2 Beaters	Organising the line of beaters on the day.
3 Pickers-up	Ensuring that there are people with well trained dogs at each drive, behind the line of guns, to humanely retrieve shot and wounded game.
4 Stops	Making sure that these are strategically and correctly sited at each drive.
5 Storage and sale of game	The gamekeeper must ensure that the shot game is handled and stored correctly, thus guaranteeing that, when it is sold to the game-dealer, it commands a realistic price.
POACHING AND TRESPASS	Disturbance of game must be kept to a minimum. It is important that game is not subjected to a lot of human disturbance, and it is the gamekeeper's job to ensure that this is kept to an absolute minimum.

Appendix 1

OFFICIALLY DESIGNATED AREAS OF LANDSCAPE OR CONSERVATION VALUE

SITES OF SPECIAL SCIENTIFIC INTEREST (S.S.S.I.s)

Over the past thirty years the Nature Conservancy Council (N.C.C.), the official body responsible for nature conservation, has identified areas of special scientific interest throughout Great Britain that are judged to be of special importance for their wildlife or geological or physiographical features. Many of the N.C.C. responsibilities are now managed by various new government conservation agencies.

The prime purpose of S.S.S.I.s is to provide an objective list of areas which need to be monitored and protected. Some of these areas are nature reserves but many are not. S.S.S.I.s are subject to a certain amount of legislative protection governing their management by owners and occupiers. Shooting men considering management schemes on S.S.S.I.s should seek advice from BASC during the planning stages.

NATIONAL NATURE RESERVES (N.N.R.)

National nature reserves protect some of the country's best wildlife habitats. Caerlaverock N.N.R., Lindisfarne N.N.R., and the Bridgewater Bay N.N.R. are examples.

LOCAL NATURE RESERVES (L.N.R.)

These fall under the responsibility of a local authority in consulation with the relevant government conservation agency. Management may be designated to voluntary conservation bodies.

OTHER DESIGNATED AREAS

These include areas such as national parks, areas of outstanding natural beauty and green belts which may be set aside for their landscape features and which provide for recreation or amenity. In order to protect these valuable sites certain planning controls are applied by appropriate local authorities.

AREAS OF SPECIAL PROTECTION FOR BIRDS

These areas are set up by the minister for the environment to provide special protection for birds where it is necessary. In earlier legislation they were called Sanctuaries.

Appendix 2

CURRENT OR RECENT RESEARCH STUDIES
CONDUCTED BY THE BASC

IMPORTANCE OF
LOWLAND GAME
SHOOTING

To demonstrate and promote the environmental benefits of lowland game shooting.

TESTING AND USE OF
NON-TOXIC SHOT FOR
WETLAND SHOOTING

To help members through the Government's lead shot replacment programme.

WOODPIGEON SHOOTING
SURVEY

To show the importance of and monitor year-round pigeon shooting for sport and crop protection. (report available)

ACCESS SURVEY

To ensure the Government's review of access to the countryside does not disadvantage shooting and stalking.

WILDFOWL SHOOTING
SURVEY

To monitor the UK shooting of migratory wildfowl.

DUCK AND WOODCOCK
SURVEYS

To monitor the health and composition of wintering quarry populations.

DEER STALKING

Surveys to support members involved in deer management and stalking.

GAMEKEEPING

Surveys to support the gamekeeping profession and show its contribution to the management of the countryside.

RAPTORS AND GAME

Survey on problems to game managers from raptors. (report available)

RABBITS AND RABBIT
SHOOTING

Survey to monitor the importance of rabbits as a quarry species.

Appendix 3

PROOF MARKS

BRITISH PROOF MARKS

Because the introduction of new proof regulations and markings does not of itself render invalid earlier proof marks, guns may validly bear proof marks impressed under Rules of Proof of 1954, 1925 or even earlier. The majority of shotguns in use at the present time have been proved or reproved since 1925. Marks are normally impressed on the flats of shotgun barrels or otherwise near the breech and upon the action.

UNDER 1954 RULES
OF PROOF

The proof marks at present (1976) impressed by the London and Birmingham Proof Houses are as follows:

		London	Birmingham
1 Provisional proof			
3 Definitive proof for nitro powders	on action		BNP
	on barrel	NP	BNP
4 Definitive proof for Black Powder only			BP
	and the words	NOT NITRO	BLACK POWDER
6 Special definitive proof			SP

	London	Birmingham
7 Reproof	👑 ℛ	👑 R

Additionally arms will bear markings to indicate the maximum mean pressure* of cartridges for which the arm has been proved together with the nominal gauge (in a diamond, as ⬦) and chamber length or nominal calibre and case length. Shotguns will also bear marks to indicate the nominal bore diameter, as found at 9 in. from the breech, shown in decimals e.g. .729 in.

The Provisional, Special Proof and Reproof marks were similar to marks 1, 6 and 7, but the following different markings should be noted.

		London	Birmingham
Definitive	Proof	👑 ℂℙ	👑 BP
	View	👑 V	👑 BV
	Nitro	NP	👑 NP

together with the words NITRO PROOF

Military proof	🦁 ℕℙ	👑 BM

N.B.   The encirclement of marks impressed under these Rules

* *In exceptional cases maximum service loads may be marked in lieu of service pressures.*

as accompanied by the words Not English Make indicated proof of a foreign arm.

Additionally marks were used to indicate nominal bore diameter (such as 12 or $\frac{13}{1}$), nominal gauge (in a diamond, as ⬦), chamber length and maximum shot load. In the case of rifles, marks will indicate the nominal calibre and case length and the maximum service load of powder and bullet.

UNDER RULES OF PROOF
PRIOR TO 1904

The following Definitive proof marks were in use at the Birmingham Proof House from 1813 until August 1904.

Birmingham   View
Company Proof

These marks invariably indicate proof for Black Powder unless they are associated with the marking Nitro Proof in words.

Between 1887 and 1925 the following marks were used to denote special Definitive proof of barrels proved once only. They may appear on single-barrel shotguns and on certain rifled arms.

	London	Birmingham

CONCLUSION

Advice as to the interpretation of the marks which cannot be identified from these notes should be sought from either Proof House.

Advice as to complaints

The Proof Houses were established for public safety and are in being to ensure, by means of rigorous proof tests on every individual barrel and chamber, sound standards of materials and manufacture for all types of firearms and thus a greater measure of safety for those handling them.

To this end one of the more important functions of the Proof Authorities is to ensure observance of the regulations and to institute proceedings against offenders where the necessary evidence is put before them and is considered to justify such action.

Closer co-operation between the shooting public, gunmakers

and the Proof Authorities must result in a reduction of the risks involved in buying secondhand and foreign arms, whether through chance acquaintance, unscrupulous dealers or misinformed friends.

Information as to offences and all enquiries on proof matters should be addressed as below. The Proof Masters will gladly give all possible assistance and advice.

The Proof Master
The Proof House, 48 Commercial Road, London E1

The Proof Master
The Gun Barrel Proof House, Banbury Street, Birmingham B5 5RH

SPANISH PROOF MARKS
Proof House at Eibar

No.	Mark	Type of proof	Type of arm	Location of marks
1		Arms proved at Eibar	All	Action or frame or body
2		Definitive Black Powder	Muzzle loading smooth bore guns	Barrel and breech closure
3		Provisional Black Powder	Tubes of breech loading shotguns	Barrel
4		Definitive Black Powder	Breech loading shotguns	Barrel and action or body
5		Definitive	Long barrelled rifled arms	Barrel, frame and bolt
6		Definitive	Saloon pistols and small bore guns	Barrel, frame or body, bolt or slide
7		Definitive Black Powder	Non automatic pistols	Barrel, breech closure and body
8		Definitive	Revolvers	Barrel, cylinder and body
9		Definitive	Auto pistols	Barrel, slide and body
10		Arms made to a standard	All parts	Action or frame or body according to the type of arm

No.	Mark	Type of proof	Type of arm	Location of marks
11	BP	Obligatory nitro proof	All breech loading shotguns	Barrel and action or frame
12	CH	Supplementary or magnum nitro proof	Breech loading shotguns	Barrel and action or frame
13	E	Definitive	All foreign arms	Corresponding position to 2, 5, 6, 7, 8, 9, 11 and 12 according to the type of arm

There are other marks used, as for instance to indicate gauge, bore diameter and chamber length in millimetres, but they are in addition to those described above.

Note: Earlier proof marks not shown here may still be valid. The Proof Masters will advise in cases of doubt.

Appendix 4

WILDLIFE AND COUNTRYSIDE ACT 1981

SCHEDULE 1

Birds which are protected by Special Penalties

Part 1

AT ALL TIMES

Common name	Scientific name	Common name	Scientific name
Avocet	Recurvirostra avosetta	Kite, Red	Milvus milvus
Bee-eater	Merops apiaster	Merlin	Falco columbarius
Bittern	Botaurus stellaris	Oriole, Golden	Oriolus oriolus
Bittern, Little	Ixobrychus minutus	Osprey	Pandion haliaetus
Bluethroat	Luscinia svecica	Owl, Barn	Tyto alba
Brambling	Fringilla monti-fringilla	Owl, Snowy	Nyctea scandiaca
		Peregrine	Falco peregrinus
Bunting, Cirl	Emberiza cirlus	Petrel, Leach's	Oceanodroma leucorhoa
Bunting, Lapland	Calcarius lapponicus		
Bunting, Snow	Plectrophenax nivalis	Phalarope, Red-necked	Phalaropus lobatus
Buzzard, Honey	Pernis apivorus		
Chough	Pyrrhocorax pyrrhocorax	Plover, Kentish	Charadrius alexandrinus
Corncrake	Crex crex	Plover, Little Ringed	Charadrius dubius
Crake, Spotted	Porzana porzana	Quail, Common	Coturnix coturnix
Crossbills (all species)	Loxia spp.	Redstart, Black	Phoenicurus ochruros
Curlew, Stone	Burhinus oedicnemus	Redwing	Turdus iliacus
Divers (all species)	Gavia spp.	Rosefinch, Scarlet	Carpodacus erythrinus
Dotterel	Charadrius morinellus		
		Ruff	Philomachus pugnax
Duck, Long-tailed	Clangula hyemalis	Sandpiper, Green	Tringa ochropus
Eagle, Golden	Aquila chrysaetos	Sandpiper, Purple	Calidris maritima
Eagle, White-tailed	Haliaeetus albicilla	Sandpiper, Wood	Tringa glareola
Falcon, Gyr	Falco rusticolus	Scaup	Aythya marila
Fieldfare	Turdus pilaris	Scoter, Common	Melanitta nigra
Firecrest	Regulus ignicapillus	Scoter, Velvet	Melanitta fusca
Garganey	Anas querquedula	Serin	Serinus serinus
Godwit, Black-tailed	Limosa limosa	Shorelark	Eremophila alpestris
Goshawk	Accipiter gentilis	Shrike, Red-backed	Lanius collurio
Grebe, Black-necked	Podiceps nigricollis	Spoonbill	Platalea leucorodia
Grebe, Slavonian	Podiceps auritus	Stilt, Black-winged	Himantopus himantopus
Greenshank	Tringa nebularia		
Gull, Little	Larus minutus	Stint, Temminck's	Calidris temminckii
Gull, Mediterranean	Larus melanocephalus	Swan, Beswick's	Cygnus bewickii
		Swan, Whooper	Cygnus cygnus
Harriers (all species)	Circus spp.	Tern, Black	Chlidonias niger
Heron, Purple	Ardea purpurea	Tern, Little	Sterna albifrons
Hobby	Falco subbuteo	Tern, Roseate	Sterna dougallii
Hoopoe	Upupa epops	Tit, Bearded	Panurus biarmicus
Kingfisher	Alcedo atthis	Tit, Crested	Parus cristatus

Common name	Scientific name	Common name	Scientific name
Treecreeper, Short-toed	Certhia brachydactyla	Warbler, Savi's	Locustella luscinioides
Warbler, Cetti's	Cettia cetti	Whimbrel	Numenius phaeopus
Warbler, Dartford	Sylvia undata	Woodlark	Lullula arborea
Warbler, Marsh	Acrocephalus palustis	Wryneck	Jynx torquilla

Part II
DURING THE CLOSE SEASON

Common name	Scientific name
Goldeneye	Bucephala clangula
Goose, Greylag (in Outer Hebrides, Caithnes, Sutherland and Wester Ross only)	Anser anser
Pintail	Anas acuta

Note: The common name or names given in the first column of this Schedule are included by way of guidance only; in the event of any dispute or proceedings, the common name or names shall not be taken in account.

SCHEDULE 2
Birds Which May be Killed or Taken

Part 1
OUTSIDE THE CLOSE SEASON

Common name	Scientific name	Common name	Scientific name
Capercaillie	Tetrao urogallus	Mallard	Anas platyrhynchos
Coot	Fulica atra	Moorhen	Gallinula chloropus
Duck, Tufted	Aythya fuligulaq	Pintail	Anas acuta
Gadwall	Anas strepera	Plover, Golden	Pluvialis apricaria
Goldeneye	Bucephala clangula	Pochard	Aythya ferina
Goose, Canada	Branta canadensis	Shoveler	Anas clypeata
Goose, Pink-footed	Anser brachyrhynchus	Teal	Anas crecca
		Wigeon	Anas penelope
Goose, White-fronted (in England and Wales only)	Anser albifrons	Woodcock	Scolopax rusticola

Part II of Schedule 2 of the Wildlife and Countryside Act **has been removed** and the 13 pest species listed have been moved to a system of annual open and general licences to permit their control.

Farmers, landowners and authorised persons will be able to continue with their existing programme of pest control and to this end only a handful of general licences have been drawn up.

No individual has to apply for the licence, justify control or account for the number of birds killed or taken. Every-one involved in the year round control of pest birds will be able to carry on with their traditional practice as they did prior to the change.

SCHEDULE 3
Birds Which May be Sold

Part I
ALIVE AT ALL TIMES IF RINGED AND BRED IN CAPTIVITY

Common name	Scientific name	Common name	Scientific name
Blackbird	Turdus merula	Jay	Garrulus glandarius
Brambling	Fringilla monti-fringilla	Linnet	Carduelis cannabina
		Magpie	Pica pica
Bullfinch	Pyrrhula pyrrhula	Owl, Barn	Tyto alba
Bunting, Reed	Emberiza schoeniclus	Redpoll	Carduelis flammea
Chaffinch	Fringilla coelebs	Siskin	Carduelis spinus
Dunnock	Prunella modularis	Starling	Sturnus vulgaris
Goldfinch	Carduelis carduelis	Thrush, Song	Turdus philomelos
Greenfinch	Carduelis chloris	Twite	Carduelis flavirostris
Jackdaw	Corvus monedula	Yellowhammer	Emberiza citrinella

Part II
DEAD AT ALL TIMES

Common name	Scientific name	Common name	Scientific name
Pigeon, Feral	Columba livia	Woodpigeon	Columba palumbus

Part III
DEAD FROM 1 SEPTEMBER TO 28 FEBRUARY

Common name	Scientific name	Common name	Scientific name
Capercaillie	Tetrao urogallus	Pochard	Aythya ferina
Coot	Fulica atra	Shoveler	Anas clypeata
Duck, Tufted	Aythya fuligula	Snipe, Common	Gallinago gallinago
Mallard	Anas platyrhynchos	Teal	Anas crecca
Pintail	Anas acuta	Wigeon	Anas penelope
Plover, Golden	Pluvialis apricaria	Woodcock	Scolopax rusticola

Note: The common name or names given in the first column of this Schedule are included by way of guidance only; in the event of any dispute or proceedings, the common name or names shall not be taken into account.

SCHEDULE 5
Animals which are Protected

Adder	Butterfly, Large Blue	Lizard, Sand	Otter, Common
Bats, Horseshoe (all species)	Butterfly, Swallowtail	Lizard, Viviparous	Porpoise, Harbour
Bats, Typical (all species)	Cricket, Field	Moth, Barberry Carpet	Slow-worm
Beetle, Rainbow Leaf	Cricket, Mole	Moth, Black-veined	Snail, Carthusian
Burbot	Dolphin, Bottle-nosed	Moth, Essex Emerald	Snail, Glutinous
Butterfly, Chequered Skipper	Dolphin, Common	Moth, New Forest Burnet	Snail, Sandbowl
Butterfly, Heath Fritillary	Dragonfly, Norfolk Aeshna	Moth, Reddish Buff	Snake, Grass
	Frog, Common	Newt, Great Crested	Snake, Smooth
	Grasshopper, Wart-biter	Newt, Palmate	Spider, Fen Raft
		Newt, Smooth	Spider, Ladybird
			Squirrel, Red
			Toad, Common
			Toad, Natterjack

Appendix 5

SHOOTING A MOVING TARGET

There are several recognised methods of consistently shooting a moving target. The method outlined below is that used by the Clay Pigeon Shooting Association to coach beginners.

The C.P.S.A. approved method is based on three principles:

1 When the gun is properly mounted (raised into the shoulder), it should point in the direction in which the shooter is looking.

2 The easiest thing to look at is the target.

3 In all forms of shotgun shooting, at the moment of firing, the barrels are aligned so as to place the shot in front of the target along its line of flight. This is generally referred to as 'lead'.

The secret of successful shooting is to use these three fundamental principles to produce the correct effect.

To develop these basic points further:

1 Make sure that you are shooting from the correct shoulder and that your 'master eye' is placed directly over the line of the barrel(s); how to test for 'master eye' is explained on page 23. Gunfit is obviously also important in order to ensure that the 'master eye' is correctly aligned over the barrels. You must practise mounting the gun into the shoulder.

2 Practise looking at moving targets and pointing at them, either with a finger or with a shotgun (always empty – safety first).

3 The exact amount of 'lead' required for each moving target can only be learned by actual experience of shooting. Each individual sportsman develops his own 'picture' of bird-gunbarrel alignment at the moment of firing.

The method can be illustrated diagrammatically:

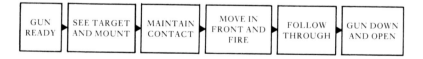

| GUN READY | SEE TARGET AND MOUNT | MAINTAIN CONTACT | MOVE IN FRONT AND FIRE | FOLLOW THROUGH | GUN DOWN AND OPEN |

As the shooter sees the bird, he will try and keep the tip of the barrels on the target as he mounts the gun. When the gunstock meets the cheek, there should be a straight line between the eye and the bird, with the barrel tip lying along that line. In swinging with the bird, the swinging action from the feet, to the hips and waist, will keep the alignment going.

Keep the swing going for a moment to establish the speed of the bird, pointing at the bird all the time, then 'move in front', fire and follow through. (Remember that the amount of 'lead' will vary depending upon the speed and range of the target.)

This sequence of diagrams is for a left-to-right crossing bird. If the bird is a right-to-left crosser, the sequence is naturally reversed.

It is important to remember the following points:

(*i*) the swing and the mount occur simultaneously;

(*ii*) there is a short period of time when the gun is pointing directly at the bird;

(*iii*) the correct 'barrel-target' picture is essential to consistent successful shooting;

(*iv*) the 'follow through' is essential in order to overcome the tendency to stop the swing of the gun on firing.

Index